CHRONICLES IN EDUCATION

A TELL-ALL BY A BLACK EDUCATOR

TRUTH TELLING IS RESISTANCE

DR. YOLANDA S PEAY

Published by Hemingway Publishers

Cover design by Dr Yolanda S Peay

Cover Edit by Hemingway Publishers

ISBN: Printed in the United States

Table of Contents

Acknowledgement

This book was not written alone. It carries the love, lessons, and strength of the people who shaped me long before I understood what they were preparing me for.

First, I would like to thank my mother, my first teacher. Your sacrifice, resilience, and unwavering belief laid the foundation for everything I have become. You taught me that education is more than schooling; it is a promise. I am who I am because you saw me first.

To my children: you are my *why*. You are the reason this work matters and the reminder of what is at stake when systems fail. And to my grandson, Noah… thank you for lighting up my life with your smile, curiosity, and kisses. You are a daily reminder of the future we are responsible for protecting.

To my husband: thank you for your patience, your steady presence, and your belief in me when the weight of this work felt heavy. Your support gave me the space to write, to heal, and to grow.

To my family, my siblings and my extended village, thank you for never questioning the size of my dreams and for celebrating me every step of the way.

To my bonus sister, thank you for adjusting my crown without telling the world it was crooked. Your quiet strength and loyalty mean more to me than words can express.

And finally, to myself: thank you for choosing truth over comfort. Thank you for writing the words you were once told to never write. Thank you for giving the words a voice when you were told to silence them. Thank you for honoring your experiences and trusting that your story mattered. Writing this book was an act of resistance, and an act of love.

About the Author

Chronicles in Education: A Tell-All by a Black Educator —Truth Telling Is Resistance is a powerful, unflinching exploration of what it means to teach, lead, and survive inside an education system that was never designed with equity in mind.

Drawing from over two decades of experience as a classroom teacher, school leader, coach, and parent, Dr. Yolanda Peay weaves personal narrative with systemic critique to expose the realities many educators and families are taught to endure in silence. From the lasting impact of educators who saw her brilliance to the damage caused by those who did not, this book traces how relationships, both healing and harmful, shape student outcomes, teacher burnout, and school culture.

Through stories of discipline, bias, leadership failures, parent advocacy, and resilience, Dr. Peay challenges readers to confront uncomfortable truths about power, race, and accountability in schools. She argues that behavior is communication, relationships are the foundation of learning, and silence only protects broken systems.

This is not a how-to manual. It is a call to reflect, to unlearn, and to lead differently. Written for educators, leaders, parents, and anyone invested in justice within education, *Chronicles in Education* reminds us that transformation begins when we tell the truth and dare to act on it.

Dedication

For my grandbaby, Noah…

You are the light that found me when the world felt dim.

Your presence reminds me why I keep fighting, for a future you'll never have to fear.

You arrived precisely when I needed you most,

And somehow, I loved you long before you ever took your first breath.

May the path I pave with this work be one you'll never need to walk.

You are my why. My joy. My forever inspiration.

Preface

This book began as a vision, one that lived with me for years before it ever reached these pages. I knew I wanted to tell the truth about my experience in education, not just as an educator, but as a thinker, a leader, and a Black woman constantly navigating systems that weren't built with my students or myself in mind. I wanted this work to reflect not only what I've seen, but what I've learned about schools, school choice, leadership, and the unspoken realities of this profession.

When I finally committed to writing, I was in a season of deep reflection. I had begun questioning the routines and roles I once accepted without hesitation. I was asking myself whether the work I was doing still aligned with what I wanted for my students, my career, and my life. Alignment became the lens through which everything else came into focus.

Around that time, I posed a simple question online: *What do you think is harder, the mental work or the physical work?* Most people answered the physical work. But I already knew my truth. The mental work, the questioning, the unlearning, the courage to move differently, was far heavier. What I understand now is that not everyone has done that work. And you cannot explain the weight of mental labor to someone who has never carried it.

This book is rooted in that understanding.

Alignment requires honesty. It requires stepping away from what feels safe, familiar, or expected, and choosing what feels true. It often means being misunderstood. But the work we do should never be about making others comfortable; it should be about placing ourselves where we can serve with integrity, clarity, and purpose. When alignment is present, everything begins to shift. What once consumed your energy loses its hold, and life begins to flow differently.

I chose education because I love students, I love learning, and I believe in the power of education to change lives. Over time, I've also learned that growth sometimes requires movement. When I have learned all I can in one space, it becomes necessary to shift, not to escape, but to evolve.

Education is a conscious choice. Those of us who serve in this field understand the responsibility, the emotional labor, and the weight our students carry into our classrooms, especially in urban and underserved communities. Our students arrive with stories, trauma, brilliance, and resilience that extend far beyond what any curriculum can capture.

I love education deeply. What I do not love are the politics, the pressure to conform to systems that prioritize compliance over humanity, or the expectation to shrink ourselves to make broken structures appear successful. Still, I remain because I believe in being the difference.

If you are an educator, I want this book to encourage you. I want you to honor what you bring to this work, extend grace to yourself when the work feels heavy, and build the resilience to grow, shift, or choose differently when the time comes. Too often, we plant seeds without ever seeing the harvest. But growth is happening, even when it is invisible.

This field is not for the weak. But if it is your choice, do not let anyone dim your light. Keep going. Your work matters.

What follows is not just my story, but an examination of the systems that shape all of ours.

"The truth will set you free, but first it will piss you off."

— Gloria Steinem

Introduction: Why This Book, Why Now

Before I became *Dr. Peay*, before I was a principal, a coach, a wife, a mother, or the founder of Peay & Associates Consultant Group LLC, I was a young Black girl sitting in an urban classroom, unaware that so much had already been stacked against me. I wanted more than acknowledgment of my potential; I wanted to be seen in the fullness of who I was.

At that time, I could have benefited from educators willing to look beyond their biases and stereotypes, educators who poured inspiration into children instead of projecting limitation onto them. Instead, I encountered adults who opened classroom windows in the dead of winter, drank alcohol from flasks at their desks, and behaved as if the students they served were beneath them.

I was raised in the inner city in a single-parent household, the youngest of three siblings. I watched my mother, a nurse working three jobs, hold our family together with grit, grace, and unwavering love. She raised me to look beyond what others thought of me. I took her word over their actions.

Some readers may expect a familiar narrative: a struggling household, a broken education system, a child left behind. But that is not this story. My mother was the reason I loved learning. Education wasn't just a priority in our home; it was a promise. A promise that if I worked hard and believed in myself, I could make a way.

My mother showed me what it looks like when an adult truly believes in a child's potential. She modeled unconditional love in ways that shaped everything I became. My family has always been my foundation.

I often joke that if I told my mom, sister, and brother I wanted to go to the moon, they'd say, *"That's great! What do you need to do to get there?"* They wouldn't question whether it was possible; they'd start celebrating before I even packed my bags. LaTonya and Duwon, I love you.

That kind of belief changes you. My mother was my first teacher, and the best one I ever had. She taught me that when you are raised in love, you learn to see possibilities where others see limits.

It wasn't until high school that I began to understand what truly separated urban schools from suburban schools. I didn't know I was receiving a subpar education because my mother, through her love, sacrifice, and presence, filled in the gaps. I didn't know I lived "in the hood" because, in my world, we were all family, and I never lacked what mattered most.

High school changed that. That's when I learned school was never neutral. It could be a place of possibility, or a place of harm, depending on who you were, how you looked, and whether the adults around you chose to see your full humanity.

I became a teacher to change that. I became a school leader to pour into children and educators whom no one was pouring into. And I'm writing this book now because I am tired of the silence that surrounds our truth.

This book has been in the making for years.

- In hallway conversations.
- In tearful teacher check-ins.
- In late-night emails with parents who felt unheard.
- In the eyes of Black students, searching for someone who gets it.

And in my own hurtful interactions, especially when my supervisors chose to protect their egos instead of doing what was right for the students they served. Their silence, dismissiveness, and defensiveness taught me just as much as the students did: that leadership without humility is a barrier to justice.

There is a fine line that is sometimes crossed when you are both an educator and a parent advocating for your child. I remember the knot in my stomach as

I watched my own son struggle in the classroom. I knew something wasn't right, yet every attempt to get support was dismissed.

When I had him tested independently, the diagnosis, auditory processing disorder, was brushed off. *"That's a diagnosis every child has these days,"* they said. He received the bare minimum: a 504 plan, implemented without urgency or care.

In that meeting, I watched adults coordinate narratives, deflect accountability, and hide behind educational jargon they assumed I wouldn't understand. The teacher was tenured. The principal protected her. And I knew exactly why, because I was an educator, too. I had sat in those same seats, and I had chosen to lead differently.

I left that meeting changed…

If I, an educator with advanced degrees and insider knowledge, could be dismissed and gaslit, what was happening to parents without my background? Parents who didn't know the system's games. Parents who couldn't decode the language. Parents who walked away feeling small, confused, and defeated.

That day, I decided my resistance would be helping parents and educators find their voice.

That decision is what led to this book. This is a tell-all, not for drama, but because truth-telling itself is resistance. I am pulling back the curtain on what it means to teach while Black, lead while Black, and survive systems never built for us. This is not a polished or sanitized version of education. This is what happens when the mic is finally passed to those who have been doing the work while being hurt by the work.

In these pages, you will hear my story, and the stories of other Black educators who have carried schools, challenged inequity, and poured into children in ways that often go unseen. These are not just stories. They are testaments.

This book is for the educator who is exhausted but still shows up. For the parent who knows something feels off but can't quite name it. For the leader who wants to do better. For the policymaker who needs to stop talking and start listening.

You don't need a cape to be a hero in education, but you do need courage. And telling the truth in a system built on your silence is one of the most courageous acts there is.

Pull up a chair. The chronicles begin now. Remember: **truth-telling is resistance.**

The truths in these pages did not begin in boardrooms or policies. They began in classrooms when an educator chose to see me. Before I could name inequity, justice, or resistance, someone planted a seed.

Chapter One returns to those beginnings.

Because every act of resistance starts with being seen.

With love and liberation,

—Dr. Yolanda Peay

How to Use This Book:

Chronicles in Education is not meant to be read passively.

This book is both a story and a mirror. It shares lived experiences, but it also asks you to examine your own—your beliefs, your practices, and the systems you are part of shaping every day. Each chapter invites you to pause, reflect, and consider how the themes show up in your personal and professional life.

Throughout the book, you will find brief reflection sections titled Pause & Reflect. These are not assignments. They are intentional moments to slow down, think deeply, and connect what you are reading to what you are living. You may choose to write, discuss with a colleague, or simply sit with the questions. There is no required way to engage.

Some readers will move through this book independently, using the reflections as a space for personal growth. Others may read it alongside peers, using the prompts to spark meaningful conversation about teaching, leadership, and equity. Both approaches are valid. The goal is not completion—it is awareness, alignment, and action.

You do not need to have all the answers. You only need a willingness to examine, to listen, and to consider what might change if we led with greater honesty, courage, and connection.

Take your time. Return to sections when needed. Let what resonates guide you.

Transformation in education does not begin with programs.

What moment made you proud to be a Black educator?

"The moment I decided to free myself from the constraints of public education and use my talents and skills in a more productive and meaningful way by founding and operating my own private school. I now have the autonomy to teach with real purpose and positively impact students' lives."

— Kenyetta Russell

CEO and founder of Learn to Thrive Education, educational consultant and coach

---

Chapter One
Planted Seeds, Rooted Purpose

Two educators changed the trajectory of my life.

Neither wore a cape. Neither delivered a speech meant to inspire. What they did was far more powerful: they saw me before I learned how to see myself.

Long before I understood policy, equity, or resistance, I learned the power of being seen.

The first was Mrs. Benjamin, a high school substitute language-arts teacher with short black hair, gentle eyes, and a kindness that radiated in a school where softness was rare. Most substitutes were either disinterested or overwhelmed, but Mrs. Benjamin looked at us… really looked at us, as if we belonged. While other substitutes focused on surviving the day, Mrs. Benjamin paid attention.

One afternoon, as I hurried between classes, she reached out and gently caught my arm.

"Hold on a second," she said, guiding me to the side of the hall.

There was no urgency, only intention. She met my gaze, pressed a worn paperback into my hands, and whispered:

"I think you're going to love this."

It was I Know Why the Caged Bird Sings by Maya Angelou.

Over the next couple of days, I read and learned that Maya was silent for five years after being sexually assaulted, yet she rose to become an icon for little Black girls like me. Each page flooded me with anger, hope, and recognition. More than anything, I felt seen. Mrs. Benjamin hadn't merely handed me a book; she'd placed a blueprint for possibility in my palms.

Later, I realized she had done something that so many educators never attempted with children who looked like me: she offered representation, liberation, and language for emotions I didn't yet understand. That book did more than introduce me to Maya Angelou; it introduced me to myself. It taught me that my voice mattered, that my story held weight, and that pain did not have the final say in who I would become. It taught me the true meaning of resistance and self-love.

Looking back, that moment was one of the seeds planted in me long before I ever stepped foot into a classroom as an educator. It was the beginning of my understanding that when students see themselves reflected in the curriculum, or simply in an adult who believes in them, everything changes. It is why I teach the way I teach. It is why I lead the way I lead. And it is one of the reasons I am writing this book now: to remind educators of the power they hold and to remind children of the brilliance they carry, even when the world tries to dim it.

The second educator was Mr. Nuwer, my high school horticulture teacher, crew-cut, National Guard sergeant, dirt permanently settled beneath his fingernails. His class was structured and predictable, the kind of environment where expectations were clear, and every student knew their role. He cracked jokes and kept things light, but the moment it was time to work, he pivoted with military precision. Something was grounding about his classroom… something safe and steady that I hadn't experienced often in school.

He was the type of teacher who saw you without announcing that he saw you. No big speeches. No performative moments. Just presence. Consistency. Humanity.

One afternoon, we were potting spider plants when he asked, eyes still focused on the soil,

"So, what are you going to school for?"

"I don't know yet," I replied, brushing dirt from my hands.

He stopped, looked me directly in the eye, firm but gentle, and said,

"You should be a teacher."

That was it. No pep talk. No explanation. No emotional buildup. Just a seed, dropped casually, as if he hadn't just shifted the trajectory of my entire life.

But something in the way he said it stuck. Maybe it was the certainty in his voice. Maybe it was the fact that it came from someone who treated every student like they mattered. Or maybe it was because he saw something in me that I hadn't yet learned to see in myself.

A month later, while touring Medaille College, I declared elementary education as my major. I didn't second-guess it. I didn't wrestle with the decision. His words had already taken root.

Mr. Nuwer passed in 2012 after thirty years of teaching… thirty years of planting seeds he would never see bloom. I was one of them. And every day I step into a classroom, a boardroom, or a school building, I carry that seed with me. His belief in me didn't come with fanfare; it came with truth. Sometimes that's all a child needs; one moment of being seen by an adult who means it.

Lessons They Never Taught Me

Armed with a four-year degree and a single month of summer training, I walked into my first classroom ready, or so I believed.

The charter school was brand-new: fresh paint, invigorating curriculum, founders from Michigan brimming with ideas. I spent hours memorizing the names of my twenty-five first-graders, printing each one carefully on bright nameplates. My bulletin boards were tight, lesson plans meticulous, teacher voice rehearsed. Everything felt perfect.

It unraveled by lunch.

None of my coursework covered a child melting down because breakfast was the only meal they trusted, or how to teach phonics while two students argued over a crayon. I yelled until I went home hoarse, convinced volume equaled authority.

One afternoon, a veteran lead teacher lingered outside my door, caught my eye, and beckoned me into the hallway.

"Stop yelling," she whispered. "It doesn't work."

That night, I replayed her words over and over in my mind.

She was right.

I had launched straight into academics without giving my students a reason to trust me or a chance to know me. I thought I was doing my job by diving into instruction, but I missed the most important part: connection.

That lead teacher didn't just check me, she saved me.

She showed me what it meant to lead with heart.

And over time, she became one of my closest friends…

She even became my daughter's godmother.

Sometimes the most transformative lessons in our careers don't come from PD sessions or textbooks, but from the people bold enough to hold up a mirror.

The next morning, I did something that went against everything I thought I was "supposed" to do: I paused the curriculum.

We played get-to-know-you games.

We shared our favorite snacks, songs, and stories.

We laughed at photos of my family, and theirs.

Slowly, the room softened.

The chaos didn't disappear overnight, but it gained context.

I began to see children, not behaviors.

And they began to see a human being, not just a voice demanding compliance.

That day, I learned something no textbook had ever taught me:

A degree does not make an effective teacher.

Connection does.

That shift changed everything. That day became the foundation for every future classroom I led, every teacher I coached, and every training I facilitated. Because I understood, relationships aren't something you add in *after* teaching. They are the teaching.

Finding Joy in the Chaos

Teaching never became easy, but once I stopped looking for perfection, I started noticing joy in small, stubborn places:

- The silent look of acceptance in the face of a child whose name I pronounced correctly on the first try.
- The handwritten note, **"You're the best teacher ever,"** on a day I felt like the worst.
- The collective gasp when a messy science experiment finally worked;
- A child frustrated from acting as the mom at home to her siblings finds comfort in learning in the classroom.
- Hearing a student call me **"mom,"** even if by mistake, and knowing that I am doing something right.

Joy did not announce itself with trophies or test scores. It whispered in ordinary moments that proved relationship is the curriculum beneath all curriculum. These flashes of light kept me steady while I learned to lead, not merely survive.

Truth-Telling as Resistance

Looking back, I now understand why Mrs. Benjamin slipped me a book in the hallway, and why Mr. Nuwer spoke a future into existence that I hadn't yet imagined, both were quiet acts of resistance. In their own way, they told the truth: that a Black girl from an overlooked community possessed boundless potential. And then, they dared me to believe it.

That belief is what I carry into every classroom I enter, every coaching session I lead, and every word I write in this book. Because telling the unvarnished truth about our students, ourselves, and the systems we navigate, is a radical act. Especially when silence is what's expected.

I could have kept teaching the same way, going through the motions without truly reaching anyone. But I saw something in my students. I wanted more, not just for them but also for myself. If I couldn't reach them, what was the point? I would've failed them the same way so many teachers once failed to see *me*.

So, I write boldly, lovingly, and unapologetically, because naming reality is the first step in transforming it. If even one sentence I write plants a seed in the mind of another educator or child, the way those two teachers planted one in me, then the resistance lives on… one honest story at a time.

The educators who shaped me were not anomalies; they showed me what intentional belief can do. Yet this belief did not begin with them. Long before integration, Black schools were centers of rigor, care, and unapologetic excellence, created by and for communities determined to educate their children despite a system designed to deny them.To understand what we lost, and what we are still fighting to reclaim, we must look back before the doors were ever opened.

✧ Pause & Reflect

Planted Seeds, Rooted Purpose

Every educator's journey begins long before the first classroom, the first lesson plan, or the first title. It begins in moments — of being seen, unseen, affirmed, or dismissed.

This chapter invites you to return to those moments and consider how they continue to shape the way you lead, teach, and respond to students today.

Our beliefs about education are rarely formed through theory alone. They are formed through lived experience. The classrooms we sat in, the voices that encouraged us, and the ones that silenced us all leave an imprint. Whether we recognize it or not, we often carry those experiences into our professional practice — sometimes repeating what helped us, and sometimes unintentionally replicating what harmed us.

Before we can transform systems, we must first understand the roots that grounded us.

Consider:

- When did you first realize that school was not a neutral space, but one that shaped identity, opportunity, and belonging?
- Who affirmed your potential along the way? Who did not—and how did that absence influence you?
- In what ways have your early experiences shaped how you interpret behavior, define success, or build relationships with students?
- What does it mean, in your context, to teach or lead from connection rather than control?

Leadership Lens:

How might the personal experiences educators carry — both empowering and painful — influence the culture of a school system if they remain unexamined?

A Small Shift:

This week, pay attention to one interaction where you can intentionally choose affirmation, curiosity, or relationship-building. Notice how small moments can interrupt patterns and create new ones.

"Unless our children begin to learn together, there is little hope that our people will ever learn to live together."

— Thurgood Marshall

Chapter Two
Segregation: Education Before Integration

Before 1954, many people of color believed desegregation would finally move the needle toward justice. They considered it progress. They were more fixated on what it said on paper. It promised equality, access, and opportunity, which was something people of color were deprived of—the resources that were denied to us for a long time.

Despite the promises written into policy, desegregation did not dismantle inequality; it merely repackaged it, disguising harm as progress. We were invited into systems that were never redesigned to include us. Access was granted, but power was not shared—and culture was not preserved. The cost of that trade-off was steep.

If you're an educator, you've probably studied Brown v. Board of Education of Topeka. In that landmark 1954 decision, the United States Supreme Court declared "separate but equal" educational facilities unconstitutional. We're taught to celebrate it, as it was a turning point that was supposed to change everything.

There would be very few people who haven't heard of Ruby Bridges. Born the same year as the ruling, she became a national symbol of courage when, at just six years old, she integrated an all-white elementary school in Louisiana. Escorted by U.S. Marshals, Ruby walked through a screaming mob, people hurling racial slurs, throwing objects, even holding up a tiny coffin with a Black doll inside. Her small frame, bowed head, and those four armed guards surrounding her captured both the ugliness of white resistance and the quiet bravery of a child too young to comprehend the hatred aimed at her.

And yet, we believed. We believed that desegregation would open doors long shut in our faces—that it would allow us to participate in spaces we had once been forbidden even to imagine. We imagined our children finally having the same textbooks, science labs, libraries, and playgrounds that white children enjoyed without question. For the first time, we believed our children would be seen for who they were—as children—and afforded the same rights long granted to white children. We were convinced that sitting side by side in the same classrooms would force America to recognize our full humanity. We focused on equality—on access to what others had—without realizing then that equality is not the same as equity.

We believed in the opportunity, and we were willing to prove that we deserved it. What we didn't realize was that we were also stepping into uncharted territory, forced to navigate spaces that were never designed with us in mind. There was no roadmap—no guidance for how to enter institutions that demanded our presence but rejected our culture. We were told this was progress, yet few were prepared for the emotional cost it required. The expectation was assimilation, not transformation. Schools were not asked to change—to reflect or respect our culture, our voices, or our excellence.

In those early days, we were navigating foreign terrain—learning the language, attempting to meet expectations, and bearing the unspoken rules of spaces that did not welcome us with open arms. We were met with judgmental glances, racist frowns, and acts of condescension—sometimes overt, more often subtle. Belittling words were wrapped in the guise of guidance or instruction, delivered as if correction were care. Our presence was enforced by law, but it was not embraced. We were granted access, yet expected to leave parts of ourselves behind at the schoolhouse door. What the majority of us failed to completely understand was the fact that Black schools, though chronically underfunded, already provided something far more powerful: equity through cultural relevance, unshakable high expectations, and a deep, unwavering belief in Black children's brilliance.

Black educators have always been more than instructors; they were the heartbeat of the Black community. They were the ones who stood in the gap created by society when it failed to protect us, the ones who believed in our brilliance before the world could even pronounce our names correctly. They were community leaders, nurturers of potential, and fierce advocates for our children's futures. They didn't just teach us reading, writing, and arithmetic—they taught us pride, resilience, and dignity.

These educators understood that education wasn't just academic, it was cultural, emotional, and deeply personal. They saw our children not as problems to be managed, but as promises to be fulfilled. They demanded excellence, not because they were harsh, but because they understood what was at stake. Their classrooms were sanctuaries of high expectations and radical care. Even when faced with crumbling buildings, hand-me-down books, and meager resources, they created miracles. They cultivated scholars, leaders, and change-makers from the soil of neglect.

Yet, in our collective push toward desegregation, a push rightfully rooted in the pursuit of equal access, we underestimated the power of what we already had. We believed we were moving toward something greater, unaware that we were being asked to trade the soul of our schools for access to someone else's idea of success. Integration didn't simply open doors—it closed many others. The cost was steep: Black teachers lost their jobs, Black students lost their cultural mirrors, and Black communities lost their educational anchors.

The tragedy of desegregation is that it often required assimilation into systems that did not see us, did not value our methods, and did not preserve the legacy we had already built. Instead of honoring the thriving ecosystems of care and rigor within Black institutions, those systems were dismantled in the name of progress.

Integration should have been about more than proximity. It should have been about power-sharing, mutual respect, and preserving the excellence already present in Black-led schools. But instead, our schools were absorbed without our culture being acknowledged, our educators were displaced, and our children were expected to conform to environments that saw their identity as a liability, not a gift.

We were expected to assimilate. Instead, we endured. We rebuilt. We resisted. And Black educators today carry the torch lit by those who came before—educating, leading, and advocating not just with skill, but with soul. When I began my undergraduate studies in elementary education at Medaille College in 1996, there were only two students of color in my cohort—and one of them was me. At the time, I didn't think much of it. I assumed education simply wasn't a profession that appealed to many Black students. I hadn't yet learned to connect the dots. I didn't yet know the history I understand today.

The Hidden Cost of Progress

I didn't know, at least not early on, that in the years following the *Brown v. Board of Education* decision, more than 38,000 Black teachers and administrators lost their positions. What was framed as progress came at the cost of professional livelihoods, cultural continuity, and communal trust. Entire communities were disrupted, not just through forced busing or the closing of beloved schools—but through the calculated and systemic erasure of the very people who had long sustained Black education.

Black educators, many of whom had achieved advanced degrees and earned unmatched reputations within their communities, were deemed "unfit" to teach white children, even as they had been extraordinary stewards of Black excellence for generations. They weren't laid off due to incompetence or lack of credentials; they were pushed out because their presence disrupted a vision of integration that didn't truly include them. In this supposed step forward, white teachers took their places, and Black children were often the only ones expected to adapt.

We lost more than jobs. We lost elders, mentors, and gatekeepers of cultural knowledge. We lost the ones who saw our children not just as students, but as kin. We lost leaders who understood the urgency of their education, not just as a career but as a calling. And while the doors to white schools opened, the heart of Black education, the communal, deeply relational, high-standard legacy built by Black educators, was quietly dismantled.

No one told us that the fight for access came at the cost of representation. In gaining the right to enter white schools, we lost thousands of mirrors—

educators who looked like us, spoke like us, understood our families, and saw our potential even before we saw it ourselves.

I didn't realize that I was a representation of what was once lost, made out to be the minority in a space my ancestors once owned. I had no idea of the weight that was about to be placed on my shoulders. I thought I was just earning a degree. I didn't understand yet that I was stepping into a legacy of resistance.

When I had to take a year off to have my firstborn, it was my mother, who had worked so hard her whole life, who borrowed money so that I could finish. She, too, became an integral part of the cause. Neither of us knew it then. We were simply doing what Black women have always done: pushing forward, sacrificing in silence, and carrying more than anyone could see.

Looking back now, I realize how significant my presence in that college classroom really was. I wasn't just preparing to become a teacher; I was reclaiming space that had been stripped from us. I remember a class I took—Educational Foundations—where we were asked to write our philosophy of education. I wrote mine honestly, stating that Black history should be taught 365 days a year. When my professor read it, she advised me to reconsider, warning that such a statement might make me less employable. I chose to keep it anyway, despite her pushback. I never really expected her to understand; my history wasn't something she tried to understand or even relate to at a basic level. But I knew then, as I know now, that my truth was worth standing by.

Representation matters, not just in theory, but in daily practice. When students don't see themselves reflected in the people leading them, it chips away at how they see their own potential.

The removal of Black educators after desegregation didn't just shift demographics; it disrupted the academic and emotional development of generations of Black children. These were children who had once been taught by people who understood them deeply, who expected excellence from them, and who affirmed their intelligence daily. In many newly integrated schools, they were suddenly placed in classrooms where they were seen as deficits, not scholars.

They were underestimated, tracked into lower-level courses, overlooked for gifted programs, and met with lowered expectations that resulted in watered-down instruction. Over time, the belief that they could not learn—or could not learn as well—became internalized, not only by the students themselves but also by the educators charged with uplifting them. It wasn't just about who was at the front of the classroom. It was about the messages being sent through tone, curriculum, discipline, and opportunity. The absence of representation told Black students, "This space is not for you." And over time, too many began to believe it.

When teachers don't believe in their students' ability to excel, their instruction reflects that. They stop pushing. They stop differentiating. They stop trying. And Black students, already carrying the burden of bias, are left to navigate an education system that neither sees nor serves them.

Instructional inequity becomes self-fulfilling. A system that assumes less, teaches less. A system that teaches less, produces less. And then blames the student for the outcomes.

This is why representation is not a box to check. It's a necessary condition for justice. Black teachers often enter the classroom with both the professional and cultural competency to challenge this cycle. We bring lived experience, empathy, and high expectations. We know what it's like to be unseen. And because of that, we refuse to let our students go unseen.

Truth-telling is resistance.

There will be people who disagree with me, and that's okay. I'm not looking for affirmation. This book is a testament to that. I didn't write it to make anyone comfortable; I wrote it to tell the truth.

For those who are open to hearing it, I invite you to keep reading.

By now, I hope something has stirred in you. I hope the wheels are turning. I hope you're thinking about your own role in this system—whether you're an educator, a parent, a policymaker, or someone who simply cares. I hope you're asking yourself, "How can I help shift the narrative?"

Because once we know the truth, we can't go back to pretending we don't see it. We owe it to our students, not just to teach them, but to see them. To believe in them. To fight for them.

Because I came to the realization that I'm fighting a battle that's gone unrecognized, uninterrupted, for over seventy years, and yet, it hasn't been given the spotlight it deserves to be dismantled.

We've grown far too comfortable letting others dim our light. Far too quiet about a system that consistently fails students of color, not because they are inadequate, but because it was never built to see them succeed.

The legacy of segregation did not disappear; it simply evolved. While the language has softened, the outcomes have not. Today's inequities are less overt, but no less damaging.

✧ **Pause & Reflect**

Segregation: Education Before Integration

History is not something we leave behind when we enter a classroom. It lives in policies, expectations, access, and opportunity. The structures that shape schools today did not appear by accident—they were built over time, influenced by decisions about who would be included, who would lead, and whose knowledge would matter.

This chapter asks us to confront the lasting impact of those decisions. The loss of Black educators, the silencing of culturally grounded teaching, and the persistence of inequitable access are not distant events. They continue to influence how students experience school and how educators understand their roles within it.

To move forward, we must be willing to look back—not to dwell there, but to understand what has been carried into the present

Consider:

- What patterns of separation, access, or representation did you observe in your own schooling, even if they were never named?
- How did the presence—or absence—of educators who reflected students' identities shape expectations for success and belonging?
- In what ways do historical inequities continue to show up in opportunities, resources, or outcomes within your current context?
- What responsibility do educators and leaders hold in interrupting patterns that were created long before they arrived?

Leadership Lens:

How might school systems unintentionally maintain historical inequities through practices that appear neutral but produce uneven outcomes?

A Small Shift:

Take notice this week of one structure—placement decisions, communication practices, discipline responses, or access to opportunities—and ask: *Who benefits from this, and who might be left out?* Let that question guide one intentional adjustment.

"Equity is not a luxury. It is a necessity for justice in education."

— Dr. Gloria Ladson-Billings

Chapter Three
The Equity Equation

As an educator who has spent most of my career in urban schools, I often find myself circling back to the same haunting question: How far have we actually come since 'separate but equal'? Have we really created equal educational opportunities for all children—or are we simply more comfortable calling them equal because they sit under the same state standards and mandates?

The real question, the one that refuses to be ignored, is this: Are our schools equitable?

Before the pandemic, I bought a home right on the border of the city and the nearest suburb. A fresh start. A new district. I transferred my sons into the neighborhood schools—my youngest into elementary school and my third child into the high school. What I walked into was a cultural shift, not just for them, but for me. We had entered a small, close-knit district where parent engagement wasn't just encouraged—it was embedded into the DNA of the school community. I remember signing up as a parent volunteer for field day, only to be told that I wasn't chosen. I never knew if it was because there were too many volunteers, or if I just wasn't the right fit. That uncertainty stung—a reminder of how tight-knit the school community was, and how easy it was to feel like an outsider looking in.

PTAs. Bonfires. Spirit weeks. Field days. School dances. Fundraisers. You name it—they had it. And I started to ask myself: What creates the conditions for this kind of engagement? What makes this feel so different from the school communities I've served my entire career?

Then came the moment that hit me hard: my high schooler's schedule. It was filled with classes that screamed college readiness—courses like Public Speaking, which I didn't even see until I stepped foot on a college campus. Courses designed not just to teach, but to position students—to prepare them to lead, advocate, and succeed.

Not too long before that, I was pursuing my PhD and had an assignment requiring me to watch local school board meetings. I was grateful for the opportunity to intern under the leadership of prominent Black women in the Buffalo Public School District—leaders who consistently put students first. Their example showed me the power of advocacy, representation, and unwavering commitment to student success. The contrast was staggering. In suburban districts, board meetings were packed. Parents attended in groups. They showed up informed, united, and vocal. They raised concerns. They asked pointed questions. They voted on motions. They advocated for their children—and they were heard.

Meanwhile, I had rarely seen that same level of visibility in the urban charter schools I worked in. Our meetings were often empty. Maybe a parent or two would show up—usually with a pressing personal concern. No united front. No organized push for change.

There are many reasons for this—and there is no judgment here. Parents in underserved communities are often fighting multiple battles: housing insecurity, job instability, systemic mistrust, and burnout. But what I can speak to is the impact of that absence. When parents aren't present in the room where decisions are made, the system does what it does best: it assumes silence equals consent.

And in the suburbs? That silence doesn't exist. Because those parents are there. Loud and clear.

Equity and Adequacy: Two Sides of the School Funding Fight

To understand how school funding continues to shape unequal outcomes, we have to talk about two key legal concepts: **equity** and **adequacy**.

Equity asks: Is the system fair?

Adequacy asks: Is it enough to meet the needs of every student?

Equity-based lawsuits argue that students in low-income districts are receiving fewer resources than those in wealthier areas—creating unfair advantages. Court cases like *Serrano v. Priest* (California) and *Abbott v. Burke* (New Jersey) exposed how funding disparities violated students' rights to equal education.

Adequacy lawsuits shift the focus from comparing districts to asking whether students are receiving what they actually need to succeed. It's not about sameness—it's about sufficiency. One landmark example is *Campaign for Fiscal Equity (CFE) v. State of New York*. In this case, the plaintiffs argued that New York State was not providing students—especially those in New York City—with the resources necessary to receive a "sound basic education," as guaranteed by the state constitution. The court agreed, highlighting how underfunded schools lacked qualified teachers, up-to-date materials, and safe facilities, making it impossible for students to meet academic standards.

This case became a turning point in how we define what schools *owe* their students—not just in funding amounts, but in the actual outcomes and opportunities that money makes possible.

In short:

Equity = fairness in distribution

Adequacy = meeting essential needs

And both are necessary. One without the other isn't reform—it's a bandage.

So Where Does the Money Come From? Understanding the School Funding Formula

Public schools in the United States are primarily funded through a three-part formula made up of:

1. **Local Revenue**

This comes mostly from property taxes. Wealthier neighborhoods with higher property values generate more money for their local schools. This creates a built-in inequality—districts with less property wealth simply can't raise the same level of funds.

2. **State Funding**

- States use formulas to try to balance out these disparities. The funding formula typically accounts for:
- Student enrollment
- Additional needs (e.g., students with disabilities, English language learners, low-income students)
- Cost of living differences across regions

But even these formulas are often inadequate or politicized, leading to further inequities between districts.

3. **Federal Funding**

The federal government provides the smallest portion of funding (usually less than 10%) through programs like Title I (for low-income students) and IDEA (for students with disabilities). While essential, federal dollars were never meant to close funding gaps—they're designed to supplement, not replace, state and local contributions.

Why the Formula Still Fails Many

Even with state funding formulas intended to "level the playing field," major gaps remain. Many states don't fully fund their own formulas, and political decisions often override student need. As a result, schools that serve students with the highest needs often operate with the fewest resources.

Bottom line: The current funding system is not neutral. It reflects—and reinforces—longstanding inequalities in housing, income, and race. That's why understanding the funding formula is crucial to any conversation about educational equity and justice.

Integrating DEI Funding into the Equity Equation

A critical piece of the equity puzzle is DEI (Diversity, Equity, Inclusion) funding. Studies show schools with dedicated DEI budgets report higher retention rates and improved student belonging. These funds support inclusive curriculum, professional development, and mentoring.

Yet DEI budgets are increasingly under threat—millions in federal and local grants are being cut. Without DEI, even the best reforms fall short. Equity makes the promise. Adequacy ensures it's enough. DEI makes it work for all learners.

Who Decides What's "Fair"?

Fairness isn't neutral—and in education, it's shaped by gatekeepers: district leaders, test creators, curriculum designers, and teachers.

Gatekeepers:

- Design tracking systems that place students of color in lower-level courses
- Enforce policies that reward conformity over culture
- Rely on biased standardized tests to assess 'potential'

Even well-meaning educators can perpetuate inequity through unconscious bias—who they call on, how they interpret behavior, and whose voices they elevate.

Unless we actively challenge the system, we reinforce it.

A Personal Lens: The Gap We Keep Pretending Isn't There

I started to see the inequities in our education system early on—especially when it came to standardized testing.

Public schools must give these tests to receive federal funds, yet most school funding comes from local property taxes. That's the real source of inequity.

As an educator, I saw firsthand how curriculum often bent under the weight of standardized testing demands. In some schools, leadership made the decision to deprioritize subjects like science and social studies altogether, arguing that students needed to focus exclusively on ELA and math to prepare for high-stakes state assessments. But when science is sidelined year after year, students—especially those in under-resourced schools—miss out on critical exposure to STEM concepts. They lose the chance to see themselves as budding scientists, engineers, or inventors. Over time, these gaps contribute to the lack of diversity and representation we continue to see in STEM careers. When access to foundational science education isn't equal, neither are the opportunities that follow. The long-term cost of these decisions was ignored: a generation of students with fragmented knowledge, denied a well-rounded education.

The impact was disproportionately felt by students of color, who already face systemic barriers that affect learning. These same students often score lower than their white counterparts on standardized tests—not because they are less capable, but because they are navigating schools that are often underfunded, understaffed, and overloaded with pressure to "perform." And yet, their lower scores are weaponized as justification for harsher accountability measures or even as fuel to deny that an "achievement gap" exists at all.

But let's be clear: the real issue isn't *achievement*—it's *access*. Access to rigorous instruction. Access to culturally responsive curriculum. Access to qualified and supported teachers. Access to mental health supports, enrichment opportunities, and classrooms where students are seen, known, and affirmed.

When we reduce students to test scores, we ignore the ecosystem of inequities that shape those outcomes. Equity in education isn't about giving everyone the same—it's about ensuring that each child has what they need to thrive. That means rejecting deficit narratives and reimagining a system where every student, regardless of zip code or identity, is given a full and fair chance.

We don't have an achievement gap. We have:

- An access gap
- An expectations gap
- An equity gap we keep pretending isn't there

Low expectations, outdated policies, and harmful instructional practices combine to create a system stacked against students of color.

When I mastered instruction, I became a performer—not a sage on the stage, but a guide. I gave students the floor, pushed them to think deeply, debate, and express themselves. I showed up as the teacher I needed when I was a student like them sitting in a classroom hoping someone would see my potential. In short, I understood the assignment.

They rose—not because they suddenly became smarter, but because someone finally saw them as capable.

But today's educational system doesn't support that kind of teaching. It wasn't built for it. And that's the real test we're all failing.

Truth-telling is resistance. And the truth is, we're still fighting the same battles our predecessors thought integration would solve. The difference is, now the segregation is more subtle, more systemic, and more deeply embedded in policies that appear neutral on the surface but create vastly different outcomes for students based on their zip code, their skin color, and their family's economic status.

The equity equation isn't just about math—it's about humanity. And until we're willing to solve for the human variable, the numbers will never add up. In other words, the math ain't mathin.

Because the truth is, you can't standardize justice. You can't spreadsheet your way to liberation. Equity demands more than metrics—it demands a moral compass. It requires looking beyond test scores and funding formulas to confront the uncomfortable truths about bias, access, and systemic neglect.

There's something deeply concerning about leaders who see numbers with perfect clarity, yet fail to recognize the students and staff right in front of them as assets.

We can't keep patching broken systems with surface-level solutions. We need courageous leadership, honest dialogue, and policies rooted in love and fairness. The work of equity is not performative—it's deeply personal. It lives in the daily decisions we make, the expectations we hold, and the opportunities we provide.

We owe it to every child to stop adjusting the mirror and start changing the reflection. Only then will the equation begin to balance—and only then will education become what it was always meant to be: a path to possibility for all, not just for some.

"Kids don't learn from people they don't like."

— Rita Pierson

Chapter Four
Love in the Classroom

I first discovered Rita Pierson while exploring YouTube on my own. I think I was watching someone else's TED Talk, and hers came up next. I sat. I listened. And I felt validated. She said the things I had long believed but hadn't yet heard spoken so boldly in public spaces. One statement stood out to me the most, "one of the things that we rarely discuss, or we won't discuss is the value and importance of human connection."

Education is, and always has been, political—make no mistake about it. Every decision, every policy, every lesson plan is shaped by agendas, often crafted by people who have never stepped foot in a classroom. But for those of us who *live* this work daily, something far more powerful rises above the politics: love. There is something extraordinary about loving what you do with your whole heart. I love to learn. I love to create. But most of all, I love children—and that love is what has always grounded me in this work.

For educators who lead with love, the classroom becomes a place of endless possibility. You love your students like they're your own. And the ones who walk in carrying the heaviest emotional baggage? You love on them just a little more—because you understand that sometimes love is the only thing standing between them and the decision to give up.

If you're an educator who doesn't believe in building relationships with your students, I'll be honest—you're already doing them a disservice. That may sound harsh, but the truth often is. Some might push back and say, "Well, my students learned just fine. They passed their tests. They followed directions." And maybe that's true. But here's what I want you to consider:

Have you *ever* witnessed what's truly possible when a student feels safe, seen, and supported by their teacher? If you've never prioritized relationships, you've likely never had the chance to witness how deeply they can transform not just behavior, but *academic performance.*

Because here's the thing—academic achievement is deeply connected to emotional security. Students don't learn well in classrooms where they feel invisible, misunderstood, or unwanted. They might perform, yes. But are they thriving? Are they engaged? Are they building confidence and taking ownership of their learning? Or are they just compliant?

Relationships are the foundation of everything. And that's not just "soft" stuff—it's science. Neuroscience and trauma-informed practices consistently show that students' brains function better when they feel emotionally safe. They retain more. They take risks. They recover from setbacks faster. They invest in the process.

And let's talk about reality: Kids try harder for people they like. They rise to the occasion when they know someone genuinely believes in them. They push through obstacles when they feel a connection. As Rita Pierson so perfectly put it, *"Kids don't learn from people they don't like."* That's not just a quote—it's the truth.

So to the educators who've never built those connections: it's not too late. Imagine how much *more* your students could accomplish—not just in test scores, but in confidence, creativity, and critical thinking—if they knew you *really* saw them. The power of your presence, your kindness, your authenticity…it matters more than any curriculum ever could.

When we talk about love in the classroom, we're not talking about being soft or lowering expectations. We're talking about reaching students on every level—emotional, intellectual, cultural, and human. We're talking about seeing the whole child and showing up for them, even when it's hard to do. Our students deserve it.

The system taught me to see cultural differences as deficits to overcome. But love—and Ladson-Billings' research—taught me to see them as assets to celebrate. When students see themselves reflected in the curriculum, when their voices and experiences are valued, they don't just learn better—they learn that they belong.

This is why so many Black educators are known for their classroom management. We're not just managing behavior—we're creating cultural bridges. We're showing students that success doesn't require them to abandon who they are. We're proving that excellence comes in many forms, speaks many languages, and draws from many traditions—exactly what Ladson-Billings envisioned when she developed the theory of Culturally Relevant Pedagogy.

Loving students means believing they are capable—even when the world tells them otherwise. It means refusing to see them only through a lens of deficits and starting instead with what they do have: resilience, creativity, intuition, resourcefulness, leadership, and heart. Even students who are up against countless disadvantages can succeed when someone sees their strengths and helps them grow from there.

Maybe there's a student selling snacks in class—they're already showing entrepreneurial spirit. Teach them about budgeting, marketing, and business planning. That child who seems to have a gravitational pull, the one everyone listens to—that's your natural leader. Help them lead with purpose. And the quiet student in the back who rarely speaks but hands in beautifully written work? That's a poet, a thinker, a storyteller. Show them their voice matters.

This is what it means to teach with love—to recognize potential in unexpected places, and to nurture it with intention. Not every student will take the same path, but every student has a path worth walking. As educators, it's our job to help them find it.

Everything I did in the classroom—and later, as a building leader—was always rooted in one guiding principle: doing what was best for students. Ego aside. Trends aside. Educational fads came and went, but one thing remained constant—love always led the way. I often got assigned the toughest classrooms, and like many Black educators, I was praised for my classroom management. But there's a catch: when you're good at it, people try to box you in. You're seen as "the disciplinarian," and your other strengths—your instructional leadership, your creativity, your vision—are too easily overlooked. It wasn't until I was more than a decade into my career that someone said to me, "What you do is powerful. You should be marketing this." That moment forced me to see my work through a different lens. The irony is, the very person who first told me my skills were marketable—someone I once considered a mentor—later became part of the reason I left a school I loved. That experience, both discouraging and clarifying, ultimately birthed Peay & Associates Consultant Group.

The truth was, I didn't even know how to explain it at first. It came so naturally that I had never thought to break it down into steps or strategies. It wasn't just a skill; it was part of who I was. It was relational, intuitive, and deeply rooted in my values as an educator.

When I began my journey in education, much of my time was spent as a substitute and an aide. In those early years, whenever I had downtime, I made it my mission to visit classrooms and observe strong teaching in action. I wasn't just watching—I was studying. I paid close attention to the methods, strategies, and approaches that worked, and I began to collect them like tools for a toolkit I didn't even know I was building.

One teacher used humor to captivate her students. She knew how to keep things light, but when it was time to get to work, her classroom shifted into gear. Her students laughed and learned at the same time—a combination I hadn't seen before. From her, I learned the power of authenticity. Another teacher diffused a brewing behavior issue not by raising her voice, but simply by walking over and making eye contact. It was subtle, but incredibly effective. I saw, firsthand, that respect breeds respect. Then there was the teacher whose classroom ran like a well-oiled machine—so structured and well-planned that I truly believed some of her students could teach the lessons themselves. Her attention to detail made learning seamless.

Little by little, I collected these moments and transformed them into my own style. I wasn't reinventing the wheel—I was learning from the greats and adding my own sparkle. And over time, I developed a toolkit grounded in real classroom wisdom, built on respect, authenticity, consistency, and cultural responsiveness. Below are a few key practices I picked up and personalized along the way.

Consistent routines and clear expectations: Seasoned teachers showed me the power of establishing routines. Simple procedures (how to start class, how to ask for help, etc.) created a stable environment where students knew what was expected, reducing chaos and anxiety. I implemented clear, consistent routines so students felt secure and focused.

Culturally responsive engagement: I noticed effective teachers made learning relatable. They tied lessons to students' lives and interests. Following their lead, I incorporated culturally relevant examples and listened to student feedback. This signaled to students that their identities were valued in our classroom.

Positive reinforcement and respect: Rather than relying on punishment, veteran educators emphasized catching students doing right. I saw teachers give specific praise ("I appreciate how Tasha helped her classmate") and maintain a respectful tone at all times. I emulated this, using genuine praise and respectful language to build a positive classroom culture.

High expectations with personal support: The best teachers never dumbed things down—they challenged students and provided scaffolding when needed. I learned to set the bar high for every student, but also to be right there offering help, second chances, and encouragement. Students rose to meet high expectations because they knew I wouldn't give up on them.

Every opportunity truly became a learning opportunity for me. By observing and asking questions, I soaked up wisdom from mentors next door. This mindset of being "always willing to grow and be the best" made a huge difference in my effectiveness. Over time, I blended all those borrowed techniques into my own unique style. The result was a teaching approach grounded in proven practices and the wisdom of experience — not just my experience, but the collective experience of great educators before me. In essence, I became an amalgam of every excellent teacher I ever watched. This willingness to learn from others kept me from burning out or stagnating. It's a reminder that in education, we don't succeed in isolation; we build on each other's knowledge. As I often tell new teachers: you don't have to figure it all out yourself. Seek out the expertise around you, and you'll accelerate your growth immeasurably.

From Teacher to Principal: Leading by Example

Years later, with classroom lessons in hand, I felt called to expand my impact and became a principal. I led with the same core belief: schools thrive when love and relationships come first. My mission was to help teachers build the same authentic connections with students that had transformed my own classroom.

I encouraged simple, powerful practices—greeting students at the door, attending their events, learning their stories, and fostering a culture of mutual respect. I knew these weren't extras; they were essential to learning.

As a leader, I modeled empathy, stayed present in classrooms, and made every decision through the lens of: *"Is this in the best interest of our students?"* I celebrated the teachers who built trust, who listened deeply, and who led with heart.

And the results? Our school culture shifted. Referrals dropped. Engagement and achievement grew. Students showed up because they *felt* seen. Educators showed up because they felt supported.

This is what I'm working to build again—on my own terms. Because I've learned: connection, not compliance, is the true engine of education.

Spreading the Vision: Consulting to Improve Student Outcomes

After successfully leading a school, I wanted to share what I'd learned on a broader scale. This led me to establish my own educational consulting company, focused on increasing student outcomes through intentional relationship-building. In this new role, I coach other educators and school leaders on practical strategies to foster trust and rapport in their classrooms and campuses. The premise is simple yet transformative: when students feel known and valued, they will achieve more. I help schools shift from a top-down, punitive mindset to one where relationships and respect form the foundation of everything from classroom management to curriculum design. My model is Academic Supports + Behavioral Supports = Academic Success.

In my workshops and consulting work, I don't believe in one-size-fits-all solutions. My approach begins with **The District Culture Transformation**

Blueprint™, a structured process designed to help schools create sustainable change from the inside out. I start by listening and gathering data to understand where the school currently stands—its culture, challenges, strengths, and opportunities for growth. From there, we move through a five-step process: consultation, data collection, strategic planning, implementation, and follow-up.

This work is not about coming in with quick fixes or top-down mandates. It's about building shared ownership among leaders, teachers, and staff so that the work continues long after the consulting partnership ends. Real transformation happens when schools invest in the people within them—strengthening relationships, clarifying expectations, and creating systems that support both educators and students.

At the heart of the Blueprint is a simple belief: sustainable school improvement begins with human connection. When schools prioritize relationships, trust, and shared accountability, they create environments where both educators and students can thrive.

Looking back on this journey—from being a novice teacher observing others, to planning the buildout of my own school, to starting Peay & Associates Consultant Group LLC—I see a beautiful through-line. Love and relationship-building were never just "nice-to-have" extras; they were the driving force behind every success. I didn't always have the terminology for it, but I knew in my gut (and later proved in practice) that teaching is about heart as much as head. Yes, we plan lessons, learn new tech tools, and analyze data, but at the end of the day, students won't care about what we know until they know that we care. My story is a testament to that timeless truth. Through my consulting work, I help other educators put love into action in their classrooms and schools. Together, we can increase student outcomes one relationship at a time. It's a mission I carry with pride, and it all started with the simple idea that every child is worthy of our best effort and our genuine care.

In education, theories and fads will always ebb and flow. We've seen buzzwords from "grit" to "personalized learning" capture attention for a while. But the core of great teaching remains constant: real relationships. My journey — from a substitute teacher soaking up wisdom, to a teacher reaching the hardest-to-reach kids, to a principal and consultant spreading a relationship-first philosophy — proves that when we center our work on love for students, everything else falls into place. Academic improvement, behavior management, test scores, college readiness — these are all byproducts of an environment where students feel loved, understood, and challenged to be their best. As educators, our legacy is not measured solely in test data, but in the lives we touch. I believe that years from now, my former students may not remember every lesson I taught, but they will remember that I cared about them.

Truth-telling is resistance. And the truth is, love in the classroom isn't just about warm feelings—it's about revolutionary practice. When we love our students enough to see their culture as an asset, when we love them enough to build bridges instead of barriers, when we love them enough to fight for their right to be their authentic selves while achieving academic excellence—that's when education becomes transformation.

✧ **Pause & Reflect**

Love in the Classroom

In education, love is often misunderstood. It is not softness, lowered expectations, or the absence of accountability. It is the deliberate choice to see students fully—their strengths, their struggles, their identities—and to respond in ways that affirm their humanity while holding them to high standards.

This chapter reminds us that relationships are not an extra layer added onto instruction; they are the foundation that makes learning possible. Students are more willing to take risks, persist through challenges, and trust the process of growth when they feel respected, known, and valued.

To lead with love in education is not sentimental—it is intentional. It requires patience, presence, and a commitment to connection even when circumstances make that difficult.

Consider:

- Who made you feel seen and valued in your own educational journey, and how did that influence your willingness to learn?
- How do you currently communicate care and belief in your students or colleagues through your words, tone, and expectations?
- When connection feels hardest to build, what barriers—time, stress, assumptions, or past experiences—might be getting in the way?
- How do you balance maintaining high expectations with creating emotional safety for those you serve?

Leadership Lens:

How does the culture of a school signal whether relationships are central to learning or treated as secondary to compliance and performance?

A Small Shift:

Choose one interaction each day this week to be fully present—listen longer, respond with curiosity, or acknowledge effort. Notice how intentional connection can change the tone of a moment.

"When we identify where our privilege intersects with somebody else's oppression, we'll find our opportunities to make real change."

— Ijeoma Oluo

Chapter Five
Pushing Back

Pushing back isn't about defiance for the sake of it—it's about protecting what's best for children. Pushing back requires clarity. It requires knowing the difference between discomfort and injustice. Not every tension demands resistance, but some do, and when they do, silence becomes its own kind of decision.

There's something astonishing about finally getting a seat at the table and realizing that even there, people still avoid naming the elephant in the room. What startled me most wasn't the disagreement—it was the quiet consensus to ignore what everyone could plainly see. The higher the table, the more polished the language, and the easier it became to mistake avoidance for diplomacy. As educators, we're taught to be flexible—it's a survival skill. The curriculum shifts, student needs evolve, the data changes daily, and school culture is in constant motion. By my third year in the classroom, I understood that adapting wasn't optional—it was required.

But leadership? That was a different beast.

When I became a school leader, I realized the game hadn't changed, but my position within it had. As a teacher, I was on my own little island. I started in 2001, fresh out of college, at a new charter school, one of the first in Buffalo, that would unknowingly shape my entire philosophy of education. In those early days, I was drowning. Observations came and went like brief storms—administrators would sweep in, check a box, and disappear. Informal walkthroughs were even more meaningless—a quick peek through the door, a nod, and they were gone. I was largely left alone to figure it out. It was baptism by fire, and I was burning. There was no roadmap, no steady hand guiding the process. Just expectation layered upon expectation. I learned quickly that competence wasn't built through observation forms; it was built in the quiet hours after dismissal, when reflection mattered more than ratings.

What I learned in college didn't prepare me for the real work of teaching. They taught me lesson plans, not how to love a child who came to school exhausted from being the parent because their mom had to work two jobs. They taught me the importance of classroom management, not how to reach a student who'd experienced trauma and had been failed by every adult in their life. They taught me learning standards, not how to see potential in places others saw problems. The gap between theory and reality was humbling. Teaching wasn't technical work; it was human work. And human work requires more than strategies; it requires presence, patience, and conviction.

I cried almost every night—not just from exhaustion, but from the weight of knowing my students deserved more than what I was able to give them in those early months. I questioned my career path at least three times a week. But I didn't give up—because my mother didn't raise me that way. Eventually, I found my footing. But just being "okay" wasn't enough. In retrospect, the educational system had failed all of us. That's when I realized that surviving wasn't the goal. Thriving was. And for my students to thrive, I had to learn how to push back against a system that seemed designed to keep us all just barely afloat.

There is so much red tape surrounding equity in education that good intentions alone are never enough. I learned quickly that if I wanted change, I needed a strategy. If you are an educator who cares deeply about the craft, you understand what I mean. Imagine having to work twice as hard to do what should already be the norm—what should be embedded in your job description—simply because leadership is not as invested in your students as you are.

Nothing about that makes sense because as soon as you decide to go against the grain, you become the issue, even if what you're doing is getting results. In schools, compliance is often mistaken for professionalism. The moment you question a directive—no matter how well-intentioned—you risk being labeled difficult. Results matter, but hierarchy matters more.

Now that I am in a different phase of my career, I understand that the real issue all along was leadership. Sometimes, the people placed in high-level positions are not wholeheartedly invested in the communities they serve. Some carry what I came to call "Superman syndrome"—the belief that children of color need rescuing rather than understanding. Their circumstances become an excuse to lower the bar instead of recognizing and building on students' natural strengths and talents. This mindset positioned leaders as saviors, not partners, and framed students through deficiency rather than strength.

Too often, these are individuals who would never allow their children to attend the very schools they lead. They drive into the city and return the same way, never truly engaging with the communities they are tasked to serve. Distance becomes both physical and philosophical. Students are reduced to data points, deficits, and budget lines rather than seen for their brilliance, resilience, and potential. Decisions are made through the lenses of metrics and money, not relationships and humanity.

In this environment, visibility can become more valued than impact, and credit becomes a kind of currency. The work shifts from doing what is best for children to protecting image, authority, and ego. And when leadership operates from that place, expectations follow suit. A quiet but dangerous narrative takes hold—the belief that Black and Brown students are not capable of excellence, only of remediation.

But children rise to environments that see them. When leadership fails to hold that vision, it is not the students who fall short—it is the system.

I began to dig into the curriculum and realized my students weren't the problem—the content was. They weren't engaged. They weren't inspired. So, I stayed late, redesigned lessons, and worked to build connections between what we were supposed to teach and what students actually needed. I started closing my classroom door—not to shut people out, but to protect the space where real teaching and real learning were taking place. I didn't want kids who could simply regurgitate information—I wanted thinkers. I wanted kids who could articulate their emotions, advocate for themselves, and navigate the world beyond the classroom.

That mindset fueled my decision to move into leadership. I believed that if I could create that kind of environment for twenty-five students, I could help create it for hundreds. I wanted systems that nurtured thinking, not just compliance. I wanted to extend that impact beyond my own classroom. But what I quickly learned was that my biggest obstacle wouldn't be the students—it would be the system itself. The barrier? Ego.

When Ego Enters the Room

Ego is one of the most destructive forces in education. It starts at the top—among district leaders and policymakers—and slowly trickles down to administrators, teachers, and eventually students. When ego takes precedence over student outcomes, schools suffer.

When ego drives decision-making, alignment disappears. Conversations become performances. Initiatives become branding exercises. And students become secondary.

Too often, I saw leaders make decisions without data, context, or collaboration. I had a supervisor who routinely rolled out changes with no rationale, just vibes. When questioned, they chalked it up to ADHD. I'm not here to shame neurodivergence, but unpredictability without accountability creates chaos. And students feel that chaos first.

Very early in my leadership journey, I realized something: ego had to be removed from the equation entirely if we were going to do what was best for kids. Every conversation, every initiative, every pivot needed to be guided by a single, grounding question: How does this benefit students in the long term? Not how it makes us look, not whether it checks a box, but what real needs are being met and what outcomes are we aiming for?

That was the moment I realized how broken the system could be. Not because we lacked talent. Not because we lacked passion. But because we had the power to do what was right for kids and chose not to. We chose the comfort of doing nothing over the decision of taking the authority. We tiptoed around the hard truths. We refused to name the elephant in the room. Silence became strategy. Avoidance became policy. And progress stalled.

Over time, I learned to choose my battles. I got quiet in meetings, knowing my ideas would be dismissed. Ironically, my silence was treated as resistance, too. It's a special kind of gaslighting—when speaking up is labeled as defiance and staying silent is seen as insubordination. I couldn't win. Not in that space.

What I struggled to understand was how so many people, with the influence, access, and authority to make meaningful change, chose instead to protect and maintain their comfort zones at the expense of student success.

But eventually, something shifted.

From Compliance to Courage

I began to understand my worth and my responsibility. I didn't want to play a part in a broken system anymore. I knew I had the credentials, the experience, and the results. But I also had something just as powerful—a voice. And I decided to use it. Not recklessly. Not reactively. But deliberately. As educators, we are responsible for more than just teaching standards—we are responsible for protecting children. That means everyone has a role in pushing back.

Just look around: banned books. Sanitized history. DEI efforts are being stripped away. Students are being denied services because they don't fit neatly into predefined boxes. The system isn't broken—it was built this way. Pushing back is how we begin to rebuild. Rebuilding requires honesty. It requires courage. And it requires people willing to risk comfort for clarity.

There were countless moments when I refused to stay quiet—when I challenged unfair discipline policies, advocated for needed resources, and spoke up in meetings where students had no voice. Most people will never know about those moments because that's the nature of leadership. It's lonely. It's thankless. It's not for the weak of heart.

But pushing back wasn't just part of the job—it became part of my calling.

When Pushback Costs You

The turning point came when pushing back cost me everything. I had known there would be consequences. I just hadn't imagined the cost would be so absolute.

I became a target almost overnight. If you're an educator, you know that shift—the moment you stop going along to get along. The cold shoulders in meetings. The sudden exclusion from conversations. The way your ideas are dismissed before you've even finished speaking. The isolation that follows when you refuse to be complicit. It doesn't happen loudly. It happens quietly—through distance, through omission, through silence.

I was pressured to implement practices I knew were harmful to my students. I was told to minimize social studies and science because they weren't on the state test—as if my students' curiosity about the world didn't matter. As if their understanding of history, systems, and their place in the world were optional. I was asked to repeat misinformation as if it were my own belief, to serve as a mouthpiece for policies I knew were wrong.

I couldn't do it.

I wouldn't betray my students like that, just to preserve my position.

So I walked away from a school I loved, a community I had helped build, students I had watched grow, colleagues who had become family. A place I had poured my heart, my nights, my weekends, my very soul into. Leaving felt like tearing a piece of myself away. Grief doesn't always come from loss you didn't choose. Sometimes it comes from the choices you make to protect what matters most.

It took two full years to heal.

- Two years to stop second-guessing my decision.
- Two years to rebuild my confidence.
- Two years to trust that choosing integrity over comfort was the right call.

And even with the pain—the sleepless nights, the financial uncertainty, the doubt, I wouldn't change a thing. I would still choose to push back. Every single time.

Because some things are worth losing everything for.

And our students are one of them.

The Real Meaning of Pushback

Every time I pushed back, I was told I was being difficult. Insubordinate. Not a team player.

But here's what they didn't understand: my pushback wasn't about being contrary—it was about being consistent. Consistent with the love I had for my students. Consistent with the equity I knew they deserved. Consistent with the truth I had committed to telling.

Pushback is resistance.

- When you challenge a policy that disproportionately punishes Black and brown students, you're resisting.
- When you refuse to implement a curriculum that erases your students' cultures, you're resisting.
- When you speak up in meetings where decisions are made about children who have no voice in the room, you're resisting.

The system wants compliance, not courage. It wants educators who follow scripts, not those who follow their conscience. But every time we push back against practices that harm our students, we're choosing resistance over resignation.

Truth-telling is resistance. And sometimes, the most important truth you can tell is 'No.'

- No, I won't lower my expectations.
- No, I won't ignore inequity.
- No, I won't stay silent when my students are being failed by the very system meant to serve them.

They called it pushback.

I called it love in action.

Because when you truly love your students, staying quiet isn't an option. Fighting for them becomes as natural as breathing. And that fight—that beautiful, necessary, exhausting fight—is what resistance looks like in the classroom.

The question isn't whether you'll face moments that require you to push back. The question is: when that moment comes, will you choose your students or your comfort? Will you choose truth or silence? Will you choose resistance or compliance?

I chose resistance.

And I'd make that choice again, and I reiterate - every single time. If you've ever been in a situation where you were made to feel as if you were doing too much because you're the person who advocates for your students—listen to me: You're not too much. You're not being difficult. You're not overstepping.

You're exactly what your students need. You're just enough to make a difference.

Through this experience, I learned profound lessons about power, perception, and personal agency. I came to understand a fundamental truth: I cannot control what others do, but I have complete authority over my own actions and responses. In the midst of the situation, I couldn't see the full picture clearly. The person in authority held a position I had not yet reached, and by default, others viewed me as the source of the problem rather than questioning the leadership itself.

What I initially couldn't recognize was the calculated nature of this person's behavior. But once I began to see through the carefully constructed facade, I inadvertently became a threat. My growing awareness made me dangerous to their carefully maintained image. Awareness disrupts narratives built on control. There's something unsettling about being truly seen when you've built your success on deception and manipulation.

This person wielded their positional power like a weapon, using it to manipulate others and maintain control. When someone can see past your performance to your true intentions, it creates an uncomfortable vulnerability for those who operate from a place of inauthenticity. The solution, from their perspective, was simple: remove the person who could expose the truth.

But I refused to be quietly erased. I switched the game entirely by choosing not to comply with the unspoken expectation that I would simply disappear. Sometimes the most powerful act of resistance is simply refusing to play by rules designed to silence you.

The system will try to convince you that caring deeply is a character flaw. That speaking up is insubordination. That loving your students fiercely makes you unprofessional. But here's the truth they don't want you to know: your "too much" is exactly what's been missing.

Keep pushing back. Keep advocating. Keep choosing your students over your comfort. Because somewhere, there's a child who needs someone willing to be "too much" on their behalf.

That's not a burden, it's a calling. And the world needs more educators willing to answer it. Resistance doesn't always look dramatic. Sometimes it looks like consistency. Sometimes it looks like saying no. And sometimes it looks like staying when it would be easier to leave.

One of the most common sites of resistance and retaliation is discipline. What is framed as behavior management is often about control, compliance, and power.

✧ **Pause & Reflect**

Pushing Back

There are moments in every educator's journey when something does not sit right—when a policy, practice, or expectation conflicts with what we know is best for students. These moments test not only our professional judgment, but also our courage.

Pushing back is rarely comfortable. It can bring uncertainty, isolation, or the fear of being misunderstood. Yet meaningful change in education has always required individuals willing to question systems that no longer serve children well. Advocacy is not about opposition for its own sake; it is about aligning actions with purpose, even when doing so is difficult.

This chapter asks us to examine how we respond when confronted with choices between compliance and conviction.

Consider:

- When have you felt the tension between following expectations and advocating for what you believed students needed?
- What factors influence whether educators speak up or remain silent in challenging moments?
- How can resistance be reframed as responsibility rather than conflict?
- What support systems help sustain those who choose to advocate for change?

Leadership Lens:

How does an organization respond to professional questioning—does it create space for dialogue and growth, or does it unintentionally discourage honest reflection?

A Small Shift:

The next time you encounter a decision or practice that raises concern, begin with a question rather than a reaction. Thoughtful inquiry can open conversations that lead to meaningful change.

"Discipline should not be a tool for control. It should be a process that supports growth, healing, and learning."

— Dr. Monique W. Morris

Chapter Six
The Politics of Discipline

Discipline and proactive behavior management are not the same, yet they are frequently conflated in schools. One reacts after harm occurs; the other is intentional, preventative, and grounded in foresight. One is reactive; the other is rooted in prevention. When schools confuse the two, they default to correction instead of cultivation, and correction alone rarely changes outcomes. When done well, proactive behavior management isn't just about minimizing disruptions—it's about creating the conditions for learning. In the schools I've led, this meant building systems that supported both academics and behavior with equal intention. We established clear expectations for students, implemented consistent routines, and invested time in explicitly teaching behavioral norms just as we would academic content. Teachers received coaching on classroom management, relationship-building, and culturally responsive practices so that expectations were both clear and fair.

We also used data to guide our decisions—reviewing patterns in behavior referrals, identifying root causes, and adjusting supports before problems escalated. Restorative conversations replaced automatic punishments, and students were given opportunities to repair harm rather than simply be removed from learning spaces.

I've seen firsthand how a strong balance of academic and behavioral supports can transform schools. They are two sides of the same coin—complementary systems that strengthen one another. When both are implemented with intention and consistency, the results speak for themselves. Student engagement increases, classrooms become more focused, and academic achievement follows.

Achievement is not accidental; it is the byproduct of environments that honor both academic rigor and emotional safety.

Some might disagree. Some might say, *"We're here to teach, not to manage behavior."* But that response is often part of the problem. It reflects a misunderstanding of how learning actually happens.

To gain a deeper understanding of why educators can sometimes resist the heart work of teaching, we have to acknowledge the elephant in the room: many schools lack proactive behavior management systems that support both teachers and students. When those systems are absent, educators are left feeling overwhelmed, unsupported, and unsure of how to respond when behaviors arise. Over time, frustration replaces curiosity, and survival mode replaces reflection.

But here's what I know to be true: **all behavior is communication**.

Every outburst, shutdown, distraction, or refusal is a signal. It tells us that something deeper is happening beneath the surface. Behavior often reflects a need, a frustration, or a skill that has not yet been developed. It is a student's way of telling us something about what they're feeling, what they're experiencing, or what they're struggling to process.

When we approach behavior only from a disciplinary lens, we miss that message. We react instead of respond. And when that happens, we miss critical opportunities to support the whole child.

Listening requires patience. It requires reflection. It requires educators to pause long enough to ask, *What is this student trying to communicate?*

Reacting, on the other hand, requires far less. It is quicker, easier, and often reinforced by systems that prioritize control over understanding.

But if we truly want students to succeed, we cannot ignore the deeper story behind their behavior. Proactive behavior management is not a distraction from teaching. It is an essential part of it.

Because when students feel understood, supported, and safe in their learning environments, their ability to engage academically begins to grow.

And that is where the real work begins.

This is especially true in schools that serve students from historically underserved communities. These students often carry invisible backpacks filled with trauma, instability, hunger, grief, or unmet emotional needs. When they walk into our classrooms, they're not just bringing notebooks and pencils; they're bringing life experiences that affect how they learn, how they relate, and how they behave. Those experiences do not disappear at the classroom door. They shape attention, impulse control, trust, and resilience.

Unfortunately, too many school systems are quick to punish what they don't understand. Too many systems default to punishment when understanding would require deeper work. Instead of asking *"What happened to this child?"* we ask *"What's wrong with this child?"* That subtle shift in language carries enormous consequences. And that framing, rooted in bias and deficit thinking, leads to disproportionate discipline, exclusion, and lost learning time. We cannot teach content effectively if we ignore the context students are navigating.

As educators, we must shift our mindset. We're not just here to deliver curriculum; we're here to create environments where students feel safe enough to learn. That means seeing behavior as a form of communication, not a character flaw. It means understanding that regulation comes before rigor. And it means recognizing that every moment of misbehavior is also a moment of opportunity: to build trust, to model empathy, and to teach students the skills they may not yet have.

Disrupting the School-to-Prison Pipeline: A Call for Justice in Discipline

The school-to-prison pipeline isn't just a theory; it's a reality. It describes a disturbing national trend in which school policies and practices funnel students, especially Black and Brown students, out of classrooms and into the criminal justice system. And the pipeline often begins with discipline.

Disproportionate Discipline for Black Students

Black students are suspended and expelled at significantly higher rates than their white peers for the same infractions. The data is undeniable:

- Black boys are nearly four times more likely to be suspended than white boys.
- Black girls, while often overlooked in conversations about discipline, are the most disproportionately suspended group relative to their enrollment. They are six times more likely to be suspended than white girls.

This disparity cannot be explained by behavior alone. It reflects systemic bias.

When Grace Is Withheld: Black Boys and the Void of Representation

When it comes to Black boys, the weight of systemic neglect is just as heavy. That weight shows up in discipline data, in staffing patterns, and in the daily interactions that shape a child's sense of belonging. I've seen the direct impact of the absence of Black male educators in our schools. Many of our young Black boys are desperately searching for someone who looks like them, understands their cultural cues, and can speak to their pain without judgment. Too often, they're misunderstood, mischaracterized, and disciplined without ever being heard. They're not consistently afforded the same patience or grace.

What's often labeled as defiance is sometimes just grief. What's labeled as apathy is often fear, trauma, or protection. Without representation in leadership, teaching staff, and support systems, Black boys are left to navigate an environment that rarely affirms them. They're expected to conform to a standard that doesn't reflect their reality, and are punished when they cannot or will not comply.

I've watched young boys shrink under the weight of labels—labels that follow them long after the incident that assigned them. Labels, such as: aggressive, disruptive, unmotivated, long before they've even had the chance to define who they are. Instead of mentors, they're handed referrals. Instead of support plans, they're given suspensions. And it's not just demoralizing, it's dangerous.

Because when we fail to see our Black boys as children, as learners, and as individuals worthy of care, we begin to prepare them not for college or careers, but for confinement.

Representation matters because it offers a mirror and a roadmap. It says, "You belong here. You can lead. You are not a problem to be fixed—you are a person to be understood." Black boys need to see themselves reflected in the adults guiding them—not just to feel safe, but to believe that they, too, are capable of greatness. They deserve mentors who will not just discipline them, but uplift them. Who will not just demand respect, but model it.

Affirmation is not favoritism. Equity is not indulgence. It is a responsibility. Until that is our standard—not the exception—our schools will continue to fail them.

If we are honest, this is not a question of awareness; it is a question of will. The patterns are visible. The disparities are documented. The stories are lived every single day in our classrooms. The issue is not whether Black boys are capable; it is whether our systems are willing to create conditions that recognize and nurture that capability.

When affirmation is absent, discipline becomes the loudest voice in a child's educational experience. When representation is scarce, isolation grows. And when expectations are shaped by bias rather than belief, potential is quietly diminished. We cannot continue to respond to the symptoms while ignoring the structure that produces them.

If we want different outcomes, we must be willing to confront the assumptions that guide our practices. We must examine who is at the table, whose voices are amplified, and whose experiences are dismissed. Real equity requires more than policy statements; it requires courage, intentionality, and sustained commitment.

Because the future of Black boys cannot hinge on luck, exception, or individual heroics, it must be built into the very fabric of how our schools operate.

Adultification of Black Girls

Educators and school staff often perceive black girls as older, less innocent, and more responsible than they actually are—a phenomenon known as adultification bias. This leads to:

- Harsher discipline for minor infractions.
- Fewer opportunities for emotional support or counseling.
- Expectations to "know better" or "handle it" instead of being nurtured.

This distorted view strips Black girls of their childhood and punishes them for being assertive, emotional, or simply different from white cultural norms.

Adultification bias does more than distort perception—it alters response. When Black girls are seen as older, tougher, or inherently more resilient than they are, their needs are minimized, and their humanity is overlooked. Their vulnerability is questioned. Their emotions are scrutinized rather than supported. And their mistakes are treated as character flaws instead of developmental moments.

When we deny Black girls the grace of childhood, we deny them space to grow, to err, to explore identity without penalty. We ask them to carry maturity before they have had the opportunity to experience innocence. We interpret confidence as defiance. We interpret self-advocacy as aggression. And in doing so, we reinforce the very inequities we claim to challenge.

This is not simply about discipline; it is about perception. And perception, left unchecked, shapes outcomes. If we are committed to equity, we must be willing to interrogate the lenses through which we view Black girls—because how we see them determines how we treat them, and how we treat them shapes who they are allowed to become.

A Personal Reflection: The Weight We Carry

As a Black woman, I know all too well what it feels like to carry the weight of the world on my shoulders—and to be expected to carry it with grace, without complaint, and without rest. I've often wondered, "Who signed me up for this?" There's a strong possibility that the assignment was handed to me so early in life that I didn't even realize I had the option to decline. It's a burden many Black women know intimately: to be the nurturer, the problem-solver, the cultural translator, the one who "has it all together." But beneath the polished exterior is often exhaustion, and behind the strength is a quiet longing for someone to see the weight and say, "You don't have to carry all of this alone."

Strength becomes identity long before it becomes choice. This burden is amplified in education, where unspoken assumptions often inflate expectations of Black women. We are expected to handle every behavioral challenge, connect with every student in crisis, and support our colleagues emotionally, all while being exemplary teachers, coaches, or leaders. When you do your job well, it becomes the expectation. But excellence shouldn't mean exploitation.

I've watched teachers shy away from hard conversations with students they don't understand, not because they're incapable, but because they're unwilling. It's easier to point the finger at the student than to examine the inequalities both inside and outside the classroom. It's more comfortable to label the child "defiant" than it is to interrogate the ways our system has failed them long before they ever stepped foot in a classroom.

But those of us who live this experience cannot afford to look away. We see the connection between discipline, race, and justice clearly. And we understand that real change does not come from punishment—it comes from presence, empathy, accountability, and the courage to tell the truth. Presence is not passive. Empathy is not weakness. Truth-telling is not aggression. It is leadership.

From Suspension to System Involvement

The more students are removed from the classroom, the more they fall behind academically. But the stakes are even higher than missed lessons. Suspension and expulsion increase the likelihood of:

- Dropping out of school
- Becoming involved with law enforcement
- Entering the juvenile justice system

What starts as an overreaction to a behavioral issue can end in a child being criminalized—especially when school resource officers are involved in routine discipline.

Exclusion is never neutral. Each removal from the classroom widens the gap between a student and the learning community they are meant to be part of. Over time, that gap becomes more than academic—it becomes relational, emotional, and structural. A student who is repeatedly pushed out begins to internalize the message that they do not belong.

When discipline shifts from correction to exclusion, schools risk becoming entry points into systems far removed from education. What begins as a behavioral response too often escalates into legal involvement, especially in environments where law enforcement is embedded in routine school discipline. The line between school consequences and criminalization becomes dangerously thin.

If we are serious about interrupting these outcomes, we must examine not only how often we remove students, but why removal has become such a common response. Because every time a child is sent out instead of supported, we are deciding their trajectory. And trajectories, once set in motion, are not easily redirected.

It's Not About "Bad Kids"

This isn't about "bad behavior." It's about a system that interprets the behavior of Black students through a lens of suspicion and control. A system that reacts instead of responds. That punishes instead of supports.

We must stop confusing compliance with learning and discipline with dignity.

What Can Schools Do?

- Implement restorative practices that prioritize relationship-building, repair, and student voice.
- Train all staff in implicit bias and culturally responsive practices.
- Track discipline data by race and gender, and ask hard questions when patterns emerge.
- Center student well-being in all policies and procedures.
- Replace exclusionary discipline with supportive interventions like SEL, trauma-informed care, and mental health services.

Students living in poverty or navigating unstable home environments are often in survival mode. They come to school carrying trauma, and trauma changes how the brain works. It's not just a matter of poor choices; it's a matter of survival instinct. Fight, flight, or freeze—it shows up in classrooms every day. And if educators don't understand the impact of trauma, we risk criminalizing behaviors that are really cries for help.

That's where relationships come in. Safe, supportive school environments begin with understanding. When staff know their students, their communities, and the context they walk into every day, behavior becomes something we respond to with care, not just punishment.

But this shift requires something uncomfortable: we have to look inward. We have to examine the biases we bring with us into the classroom, how we perceive behaviors, whose "disruption" we notice most, and whether our responses are equitable. Too often, Black and brown students are disciplined more harshly for the same behaviors as their white peers. As a leader, I found myself having to confront the bias of teachers more often than I'd like to say. If students know that you don't like them, that's a problem. No student should ever feel that, even if an educator is struggling with their own feelings. There are times when you may need to adjust the way you address a behavior based on a student's history or needs, but there is no reason why a particular student should get punished more harshly because of an educator's bias. The school-to-prison pipeline is real. And as leaders, if we're not actively interrupting these patterns, we become complicit in perpetuating them.

So why do schools continue to lean on outdated, reactive discipline policies? Because they're easy. They're fast. They don't require reflection or long-term investment. But they're not effective. Band-aid solutions won't heal deep wounds. And sending a student out of class without ever addressing the root cause of the behavior just ensures it'll happen again.

Convenience should never outweigh impact.

Let's dig into another culprit: low expectations. As a leader, I knew we needed to shift the narrative, and that shift began with mindset. I worked with many phenomenal educators who believed deeply in their students. They worked tirelessly, held students to high standards, and consistently produced strong results because they believed in their ability to move students forward. Their classrooms were proof that when expectations are high and support is strong, students rise to meet the challenge.

But I also encountered moments where expectations had quietly been lowered. Not because teachers didn't care, but because somewhere along the way they had stopped believing that students could reach higher. That belief can creep in slowly—through frustration, repeated challenges, or years of working within systems that normalize struggle rather than possibility.

One of the most important messages I pushed as a leader was simple: students will meet the bar you set. Raise it, and they will stretch. Lower it, and they will shrink.

The most dangerous phrase I heard in meetings was, "These kids can't..." Because every time we completed that sentence, we were building walls instead of bridges. We were choosing limitation over liberation.

And once a system begins to believe in limitations, it quietly begins to reproduce them.

We aligned expectations across the school, and we raised them. We shifted our focus from punishment to positive reinforcement. I noticed how many teachers were hyper-focused on minor misbehaviors, unintentionally ignoring the students doing the right thing. And guess what happened? The students who craved attention began acting out—because it worked.

When we began highlighting and celebrating positive behavior, everything changed. Teachers began looking for what students were doing right and students responded.

We also brought data into the equation. Just like we used academic data to drive instruction, we used behavioral data to identify trends, track progress, and hold ourselves accountable. We celebrated growth, no matter how small. We built in systems to reward wanted behaviors, and we built relationships intentionally: circles, restorative conversations, and class discussions about real-life issues. Teachers became partners in behavior planning. Students became agents in their own growth.

Yes, I've heard the criticisms. I've been in the rooms where people argue that this work doesn't "really work." But I've seen it. I know it does. That's not to say suspensions don't have their place, but they should never be the first resort. We owe it to our students to try every tool in our toolbox before we push them out.

Proactive behavior management is systematic. It's intentional. But more than that, it's grounded in love—love for the profession, love for the students, and a belief in the power of relationships to change lives.

Discipline, when misused, becomes a tool to maintain the status quo. It becomes a way to silence students who don't fit into a narrow mold of compliance. It becomes a barrier to equity. But it doesn't have to be that way.

Going against the grain—resisting these outdated norms—is possible. Even as a classroom teacher, you have the power to shift your culture. Your classroom can be a space of healing, not harm. A space where students are taught, not punished into submission. A space where expectations are high, and support is higher.

Pushing back is resistance. And resistance, in this case, is an act of love.

When discipline is rooted primarily in control, it shifts the focus from growth to compliance. Students begin to view authority as something to fear rather than trust, and trust is the foundation of every meaningful relationship in a school community. Once that trust is compromised, relationships begin to fracture. And when relationships fracture, learning does not simply slow—it becomes guarded, transactional, and surface-level. Students may comply, but they do not engage. They may sit quietly, but they do not invest. True learning requires safety, connection, and mutual respect.

Sustainable change does not emerge from tightening rules or increasing consequences. It emerges from strengthening relationships—relationships that affirm dignity, cultivate accountability, and create space for both challenge and support. Systems can mandate structure, but only relationships cultivate belonging.

✧ **Pause & Reflect**

The Politics of Discipline

Discipline in schools is often presented as a matter of rules and consequences, yet it is deeply influenced by perception, power, and belief. The way adults interpret behavior—and the responses that follow—send powerful messages to students about belonging, fairness, and trust.

This chapter challenges us to reconsider the purpose of discipline. Is it meant to control, or to teach? To remove, or to restore? Many traditional approaches focus on compliance, but lasting growth happens when discipline is grounded in understanding, accountability, and relationship.

Examining discipline practices requires honesty. It asks educators and leaders to look beyond behavior and consider the conditions, assumptions, and systems that shape how decisions are made.

Consider:

- What messages about discipline did you receive as a student, and how might those experiences influence your responses today?
- When have you seen behavior addressed in ways that prioritized punishment over understanding?
- How do discipline practices in your setting impact students differently, and what patterns might deserve closer attention?
- What would it look like for discipline to focus on learning and restoration rather than exclusion?

Leadership Lens:

How do policies, data, and adult beliefs interact to shape discipline outcomes—and what might need to change to ensure responses are equitable and growth-centered?

A Small Shift:

In your next challenging interaction, pause to ask one additional question before responding. A moment of curiosity can shift the outcome from reaction to understanding.

"I've been a school mom to so many people, and it truly brings me joy. I love on them through it all. I give them rough love when they need to straighten up. They know they will hear my mouth when I am disappointed. I hype them up when I see that they are making changes. I celebrate the little things. I pay attention to details."

— Abena Griffin-Hall

Educator

Chapter Seven
Saving Students One Relationship at a Time

Introduction: Why Relationships Matter More Than Ever

Relationships are the foundation of almost everything we do that involves human connection—and in education, they are essential. As a teacher, Early in my career, I made the decision to be intentional about building relationships with students from day one. Not halfway through the year when problems appeared. Not after a crisis forced my hand. From the very beginning. I didn't start with curriculum maps or behavior charts. I started with names. With eye contact. With listening more than I spoke. I paid attention to who walked in loudly and who slipped in unnoticed. Who avoided sitting near others? Who watched the door more than the board? Day one wasn't about establishing dominance—it was about establishing safety. Before I taught a single lesson, I wanted students to know that I saw them.

Intentionality meant consistency. Greeting them every morning. Following through on what I said I would do. Correcting privately instead of performing discipline publicly. Protecting dignity at all costs. Relationships are not built through grand gestures; they are built through predictable presence.

"People raised on love see things differently than those raised on survival." – Joe Marino.

For those who have never experienced the transformative power of a positive adult-student relationship, this work can be dismissed as "emotional" or secondary to academics. But care, when done well, is systematic. It is structured. It is learning how to pronounce every name correctly and refusing to shorten it for convenience. It is noticing when a student's energy shifts before their grades do. It is correcting without humiliation and making sure every student hears their name spoken positively.

This work requires discipline. You cannot apply it selectively to the students who are easiest to love. It must extend to the quiet ones, the defiant ones, the exhausted ones—and especially the ones who test you. Genuine care is not performative. It is consistent, boundaried, and intentional. Healthy boundaries sustain relationships; burnout destroys them. And when educators burn out, students lose the very consistency that builds trust.

For some students, relationships are the deciding factor between engagement and withdrawal between confidence and apathy. Without relationships, you may get compliance—but you will not get trust. You may get quiet—but not learning. Students can perform tasks without experiencing belonging, but performance without connection is fragile. It cracks under pressure.

Classrooms built on control may appear orderly, but only those built on relationships truly feel safe.

Let me be clear: I am not here to say that I saved students. That a narrative centers the adult and erases the agency of the child. Students do not need rescuing—they need recognition. Many of them have been navigating complex responsibilities and hardships long before entering our classrooms. What they are looking for is not a savior, but an adult who sees their strength and refuses to reduce them to their circumstances.

When students feel psychologically safe, their brains shift out of survival mode. A child in fight-or-flight is not refusing to learn—their body is refusing to relax. Relationship lowers threat perception. When students feel safe, their nervous systems settle. And when their nervous systems settle, learning becomes possible.

Safety is the prerequisite for scholarship.

There were moments early in my career when I misread silence as disrespect or guardedness as defiance. Students taught me to slow down, to ask before assuming, to listen without preparing my response. Building relationships did not just change students—it changed me.

Growth in the classroom is never one-sided.

Our students come with cultural wealth that cannot be measured on standardized tests, multilingual skills, emotional intelligence, adaptability, and leadership, developed in home and community. These are not obstacles to overcome—they are assets to build upon. . When we ignore them, we narrow the definition of success. When we honor them, we widen it.

The relationship-building I advocate for is about partnership, not rescue. Partnership means shared ownership of growth. It means asking students what they need instead of assuming we already know. It means guiding while also learning.

Showing up to school is not neutral for some students—it is an act of courage. Courage to enter spaces where they may not always feel understood. Courage to balance academic expectations with responsibilities at home. Our job is not to fix them. Our job is to create conditions where their existing resilience can flourish.

When you truly know your students, something shifts. You reach them in ways that textbooks never taught you. You anticipate struggles before they escalate. You recognize patterns long before they become problems.

This awareness does not come from data reports. It comes from presence.

Public correction may produce compliance, but it rarely produces growth. Dignity must never be collateral damage in the name of classroom management. Students remember how they were treated long after they forget what they were corrected for.

Influence replaces intimidation. And when trust is in place, learning follows.

The change rarely looks dramatic. It shows up quietly—in a completed assignment that once would have been blank. In a raised hand that trembles but stays up. In eye contact that lasts a second longer than it used to.

The student who once resisted begins to engage—not because they suddenly changed, but because they decided you were safe enough to try.

Learning is, at its core, a risk.

One adult's consistent belief can change a trajectory. Not empty encouragement, belief backed by action, expectations paired with support, and a refusal to give up on possibility.

Sometimes belief becomes the mirror through which a student finally recognizes their own capacity.

Barriers to Relationship Building

Building relationships with students is a cornerstone of effective teaching, but that doesn't mean it's always easy—or even encouraged—in some educational environments. There are many barriers that can prevent meaningful connections from forming between educators and students, even when the intention is there. If we don't name those barriers, we risk overlooking the very things that keep us disconnected.

1. Bias and Assumptions

One of the most insidious barriers to relationship building is unconscious bias. Some educators, often unintentionally, carry assumptions about students based on race, socioeconomic status, language, behavior, or family background. These assumptions shape daily interactions—who is seen as "capable," "difficult," "gifted," or "trouble." When we begin with a deficit lens, we limit the potential for an authentic relation. Students can sense this immediately, and many will disengage before a relationship even has the chance to form.

Addressing bias requires reflection, not defensiveness. It means asking yourself hard questions: Who do I call on most often? Who do I correct most quickly? Whose behavior do I interpret as confidence—and whose as defiance? Growth begins when we become curious about our own patterns. Awareness is not an accusation; it is an invitation to do better.

2. Time Constraints

Educators are stretched thin. Between academic demands, meetings, assessments, paperwork, and managing behaviors, finding time to connect with students on a human level can feel like a luxury. As a result, the relationship is often treated as an afterthought rather than a priority. Yet, strong relationships actually save time in the long run, leading to fewer disruptions, fewer misunderstandings, and greater student engagement. When trust is established, more time can be spent on learning.

Connection does not always require more time; it requires intentional use of the time you already have. A thirty-second check-in at the door. A brief follow-up after class. A moment of listening without multitasking. Relationship building is not another task added to your list; it is the foundation that makes every other task more effective.

3. Academic Supports + Behavior Supports = Student Success

We spend a great deal of time training educators to unpack standards, align curriculum, and analyze data. Yet we spend far less time preparing them to build authentic relationships. Many teachers genuinely want to connect with their students but don't feel equipped to do so—especially when working with students whose lived experiences differ from their own. Relationship building is treated as something that should come naturally, when in reality, it is a skill that requires intentional development.

Just as we model reading strategies and problem-solving processes, we must also model how to build trust, repair harm, and communicate with empathy. Schools that invest in relational training send a clear message: connection is not secondary to achievement—it is central to it. When educators are supported in developing these skills, instead of guesswork, relationships become a reliable part of the learning environment, rather than a matter of chance.

4. Staff Turnover and Consistency

In schools with high staff turnover or frequent leadership changes, students often become hesitant to trust. Why open up to someone who might not be there next month? For students who have already experienced instability at home or in their community, constant shifts in the adults around them reinforce the belief that people don't say. This creates a significant barrier to forming meaningful relationships. Many students will test boundaries simply to see if whether you are willing to remain present and committed.

Consistency, then, becomes a form of proof. Showing up every day, keeping your word, and maintaining steady expectations communicates more than promises ever could. Students who have experienced instability do not respond to speeches about trust—they respond to patterns of reliability. Over time, consistency becomes credibility.

5. Fear of Vulnerability

Building relationships requires vulnerability—on both sides. Yet, for many educators, vulnerability feels risky. Some fear that caring too deeply will lead to emotional exhaustion or burnout. Others were taught that professionalism means keeping firm boundaries, maintaining emotional distance, and never letting students see anything personal. But here's the truth: real connection doesn't happen behind a wall. It happens in the moments where empathy, compassion, and authenticity are present.

Vulnerability in education does not mean oversharing—it means being human. It means admitting when you make a mistake. It means acknowledging when a day was hard. It means allowing students to see that growth is ongoing, even for adults. When educators model healthy vulnerability, they normalize it for their students. And in that space, connection deepens.

Students need to see that you're human. They need to see you laugh, hear you admit when you're wrong, and feel your genuine concern for their well-being.

If you're unwilling to let your guard down for them, how can you expect them to do it for you? Vulnerability isn't weakness—it's the bridge to trust. And when students trust you, everything changes: their engagement, their behavior, their effort, and their belief in themselves.

Vulnerability isn't oversharing—it's authenticity. When educators show up as their full selves, students feel safe enough to do the same.

6. Behavior Misinterpretation

Challenging behaviors are rarely random—they're often signals of unmet needs, unresolved trauma, or breakdowns in communication. Yet too often, educators internalize these behaviors, labeling students as disrespectful, defiant, or disruptive without taking the time to understand what's beneath the surface. When we do this, we miss a powerful opportunity to dig deeper and support our students in ways that truly matter.

The shift begins with a simple but essential reframing: Instead of asking, "What's wrong with this student?" we must ask, "What happened to this student—and how can I support them?" This mindset shift is not just about empathy—it's about equity. It challenges the systems of discipline that disproportionately harm our most vulnerable students, particularly those from marginalized communities.

It also calls for a more intentional, proactive approach to behavior management. Traditional discipline models wait for the problem, then punish it. But reactive systems don't teach students the skills they lack—they just penalize them for not having them. Proactive behavior management anticipates needs, strengthens skills, builds trust, and prioritizes relationships before conflict ever begins. When we lead with intention, not reaction, we create classrooms that are not only safer and calmer—but more humane.

This approach also requires us to separate identity from behavior. A student is not defiant—they may be overwhelmed. A student is not disrespectful—they may be dysregulated. A student is not lazy—they may be discouraged. When we attach permanent labels to temporary behaviors, we close doors that could have remained open. But when we view behavior as communication, we respond with curiosity instead of condemnation. And curiosity creates space for growth.

7. Institutional Culture

Some school cultures prioritize compliance over connection. They value silence more than dialogue and enforce control instead of encouraging collaboration. In these environments, educators are often—whether directly or indirectly—discouraged from forming deep, authentic relationships with students. The focus shifts to behavior charts, suspension data, and punishment metrics rather than emotional safety, belonging, and trust. The message becomes clear: discipline matters more than connection.

When this becomes the dominant narrative, educators feel pressured to prioritize optics over impact. Classrooms must look controlled, data must look improved, and disruptions must be minimized—sometimes at the expense of understanding. Teachers who lean into relationship-building may even be labeled as "too soft" or "not rigorous enough." Over time, this creates a culture where fear of judgment outweighs the freedom to teach with humanity.

Institutional culture doesn't just shape student behavior—it shapes educator behavior, too.

But our students are not factory workers. They are not meant to be molded into uniform outputs. They arrive in our classrooms with diverse talents, voices, thoughts, and dreams—many of which fall outside the bounds of what's traditionally celebrated in schools. And that's exactly why they matter. Instead of trying to force students into rigid molds, we should be asking: why would we want them to fit in when they were born to stand out?

Institutional culture determines what gets rewarded and what gets overlooked. Do we celebrate creativity as much as compliance? Do we honor emotional intelligence alongside academic performance? Do we value leadership that looks different from the traditional mold? When schools broaden their definition of success, students who once felt invisible begin to recognize that there is space for them to thrive without shrinking who they are.

Culture is not accidental—it is constructed. And if it was constructed, it can be reconstructed.

Breaking Through the Barriers

During a segment of Controversial Conversations with Dr. Peay, we explored the realities of the school-to-prison pipeline. One guest shared a story that has stayed with me ever since. When asked why he never wanted to go to school, he said plainly:

"The streets welcomed me more than my teachers did."

He explained that the streets offered him something he never felt in the classroom—acceptance, recognition and belief in his potential.

That statement forces us to confront an uncomfortable truth: young people do not gravitate toward destructive systems because they love danger. They gravitate towards places where they feel seen. The streets, for all their chaos, often provide what schools sometimes fail to offer—belonging. There is mentorship. There is affirmation. There is a pathway to status. It may be misguided, but it is still validation.

When a student feels invisible in school yet indispensable somewhere else, the choice begins to make sense. In classrooms, he was labelled as disruptive. Outside of them, those same traits were interpreted as leadership, confidence and strategic thinking. The qualities that earned him discipline referrals earned him respect on the streets.

This is not about romanticizing that life. It is about recognizing that young people seek environments where their strengths are acknowledged. If we fail to build classrooms where students feel significant, they will find spaces that make them feel powerful—even when those spaces come at a cost.

Eventually—and not surprisingly—he became one of the most well-known drug dealers in the city. The recognition he longed for, he found. The leadership he possessed, he used. But the consequences shaped much of his adult life, including years in and out of prison. His brilliance was never absent; it was simply redirected.

What struck me most was not just what happened, but what could have been?

What if just one adult had taken time to truly know him?

What if someone had nurtured his leadership instead of managing his behavior?

What if the classroom had felt like a place where he belonged?

We'll never know—because we never built that bridge.

That absence of connection is not an isolated story. It is a pattern repeated in schools across this country, where missed relationships become missed opportunities, and missed opportunities become altered life trajectories.

Today, he shares his story not to glorify the past, but to interrupt that cycle for someone else.

And that is exactly why my work centers on relationship-building as a driver of student success. Policies matter. Programs matter. But without human connection, none of it sustains change. Every meaningful transformation I have seen in schools began not with a new initiative, but with adults choosing to see students differently.

Even now, years later, he chooses to share his story in the hopes that it might disrupt the school-to-prison pipeline for someone else. He wants to be the voice he never had—the bridge that helps educators see what's possible when we put relationships first, before it's too late.

This is why my consulting work with Peay & Associates focuses on relationship-building above all else. Because I've seen what happens when we get this right—and I've witnessed the devastating cost when we get it wrong. Through my work with schools, I've learned that every policy, every program, every intervention means nothing if we haven't first built the human connections that make learning possible.

Breaking through barriers is not about inspiration alone—it is about intentional disruption of harmful patterns. It requires adults who are willing to challenge exclusionary discipline practices. It requires leaders who understand that suspension data is not a badge of order but often a mirror reflecting unmet needs. It requires educators who refuse to write students off after a single mistake.

It also requires courage. Courage to advocate for students when systems feel rigid. Courage to question policies that prioritize control over growth. Courage to extend grace while maintaining accountability. Relationship-building is not passive—it is active resistance against narratives that predict failure.

Breaking through barriers is not about inspiration—it is about intentionally disrupting harmful patterns. It requires educators willing to look beyond behavior, leaders willing to examine systems, and schools willing to prioritize connection alongside instruction.

Because when relationships come first, trajectories change.

Every day we walk into a classroom, we make a choice: to be another authority figure, or to be a steady presence who helps a young person see what is possible.

In a system that has too often predicted failure, choosing to build authentic relationships is more than good practice—it is an act of transformation.

The question is no longer whether relationships matter.

The question is what we will do with that knowledge.

For School Leaders: Creating Cultures That Prioritize Relationship-Building

As a principal, I know firsthand that administrators set the tone for everything that happens in a school building. If you want your teachers to prioritize relationships with students, you have to model what that looks like and create the conditions that make it possible. You can't mandate authentic connections, but you can absolutely create a culture where they flourish.

Model Relationship-Building Yourself

Your teachers are watching how you interact with students. Do you know their names? Do you greet them in the hallways? Do you attend their games, concerts, and events sometime when you can? When you discipline a student, are you punitive or restorative? Your actions speak louder than any professional development session ever could.

I made it a point to be visible throughout the building—not as the disciplinarian, but as someone who genuinely cared about every student's success and the success of my teachers. I learned their names, their interests, their dreams. When teachers saw me having real conversations with students, it gave them permission to do the same.

Visibility is not about supervision—it's about presence. When students see you outside of moments of correction, their perception of leadership shifts. And when teachers experience leadership rooted in empathy rather than fear, it reshapes how they lead their own classrooms. Culture cascades downward. If warmth, curiosity, and dignity are modeled at the top, they echo throughout the building.

Hire for Heart, Train for Skill

During interviews, I didn't just ask about lesson planning and classroom management. I asked candidates to tell me about a student who challenged them and how they built a relationship with that child. I wanted to know if they saw potential in every student or if they had already written some kids off.

You can teach someone to write a lesson plan. You can't teach someone to genuinely care about children. Hire people who already have the heart for this work, then support them in developing the skills to do it well.

Heart reveals itself in how candidates talk about students—not just in success stories, but in difficult ones. Listen for language that reflects patience, belief, and ownership. The right hire doesn't blame children for struggle; they lean into it. Skill can be coached. Mindset cannot be manufactured.

Protect Relationship-Building Time

One of the biggest barriers to relationship-building in schools is time. Teachers are under constant pressure—to cover curriculum, prepare for assessments, meet deadlines, and juggle endless paperwork. In that hustle, building strong relationships with students can feel like a "nice to have" rather than a priority. But the truth is, relationships are not extra—they're essential.

As a school leader, it's your responsibility to protect time for what matters most. That's why I dedicate the first six weeks of school to intentional relationship-building. This is a critical window for teachers and students to connect—not just as teacher and learner, but as human beings.

In my work with schools, I coach educators on how to embed social-emotional learning into their daily instruction—not as an "add-on," but as part of the fabric of classroom life. It's not about pausing academic learning; it's about creating the conditions where learning can thrive.

When leaders publicly affirm that connection is instructional, not extracurricular, it removes the guilt teachers often feel for slowing down. Relationship-building is not lost time—it is leverage. The minutes invested early prevent hours lost later to disengagement and conflict.

You'll always have some teachers who resist at first. They call it "wasted time," worried they'll fall behind on pacing guides or lose instructional momentum. But when they begin to see the results—fewer behavior issues, deeper student engagement, a more positive classroom culture—they become believers. Because when students feel connected, respected, and safe, everything else becomes easier.

Through my consulting work, I partner with schools to design practical, sustainable strategies for building strong relationships—transforming school culture in ways that last.

Keep Students In, Don't Push Them Out

Nothing kills relationships faster than a punitive discipline system. When your first response to student behavior is suspension or punishment, you're telling both students and teachers that compliance matters more than connection.

I shifted our discipline approach from "What rule did you break?" to "What do you need?" Instead of automatic suspensions, we implemented restorative circles. Instead of sending students home all the time, we kept them in school and worked through the issues together whenever possible. This sent a clear message: we don't give up on our students, and we expect our teachers not to give up either.

Restorative practices require patience and consistency, but they also cultivate accountability. Students learn to repair harm rather than avoid consequences. Over time, discipline shifts from something done to students to something practiced with them. That distinction changes everything.

Provide Professional Development That Matters

Stop spending money on the latest educational fad and invest in training that helps your staff build authentic relationships with students. Bring in speakers who can teach about trauma-informed practices, culturally responsive teaching, and social-emotional learning. Give your teachers tools they can actually use and implement easily in the classroom.

But here's the key: make it ongoing, not a one-time workshop. Relationship-building is a skill that requires continuous development and reflection.

Celebrate Relationship Wins

What you celebrate becomes what your staff values. Instead of only recognizing test scores and academic achievements, start celebrating the relationship wins too.

During staff meetings, I would share stories of teachers who went above and beyond to connect with students. I highlighted the teacher who attended a student's grandmother's funeral, the one who started a lunch group for shy students, and the one who learned Spanish to better communicate with families. These stories became part of our school culture.

Storytelling reinforces values more powerfully than memos ever could. When relationship-driven actions are spotlighted, they signal what truly matters. Over time, those stories shift staff identity—from content deliverers to community builders.

Address Bias Head-On

As a leader, you must be willing to engage in the uncomfortable—but necessary—conversations about bias and equity. When disparities emerge in how students are treated—who gets suspended, who is referred for advanced coursework, who receives the benefit of the doubt—it's your responsibility to confront those patterns head-on.

In my leadership role, I made it a regular practice to review discipline data disaggregated by location, subject, time of day, and infraction type. I also looked closely at the demographics of the students involved. Then, I brought this data to staff—not to place blame, but to start honest, reflective dialogue.

If we noticed that most behavior incidents occurred during a specific subject or time of day, we had to ask ourselves: *Is this a classroom management issue—or an engagement issue?*

If we saw that a disproportionate number of Black students were being referred for discipline compared to their peers, it was time to ask: *Are we responding differently based on race or cultural misunderstandings?*

These conversations weren't easy, but they were essential. Because we cannot build authentic relationships with all students if we're unconsciously treating some of them differently. Equity starts with awareness—and awareness leads to action.

Sustainable equity work requires accountability structures, not just conversations. Set measurable goals, revisit data regularly, and commit to transparent follow-up. When leaders move from dialogue to deliberate action, trust grows—not only among staff, but among the students most affected.

Support Your Teachers' Emotional Well-Being

Teachers can't pour from empty cups. If your staff is burned out, overwhelmed, or feeling unsupported, they won't have the emotional capacity to build meaningful relationships with students.

And the truth is—many teachers are leaving the profession because of this very reality. Teaching has become a job of endless expectations, many of which are implied rather than clearly defined. Educators are expected to be content experts, data analysts, social workers, trauma-informed caregivers, tech support, behavior specialists, and more—all while maintaining high academic outcomes, managing classroom behaviors, and navigating bureaucratic demands.

The emotional labor required in the profession, especially in under-resourced inner-city classrooms, is often overlooked and undervalued. Teachers are not just managing lesson plans—they are managing the hearts and minds of children, many of whom are bringing trauma, unmet needs, and systemic challenges into the classroom with them.

Yet, in many schools, what gets the most attention are the deficits—what teachers didn't do, what scores didn't rise, what behaviors weren't prevented. This constant focus on the negative is deeply demoralizing, particularly for teachers who are pouring everything they have into the work. Recognition matters. Encouragement matters. Teachers need to know that their efforts are seen and valued—not just when test scores go up, but when they show up every single day for kids who need them the most.

As leaders, it is our responsibility to create systems of support that nurture and protect our staff. This means regularly checking in on their well-being. It means providing access to mental health resources and professional development that feeds both skill and soul. It means shielding them from unnecessary stress and red tape whenever possible—and standing by them when they need you to, just like you would for your students.

When teachers feel seen, valued, and supported, they are far more likely to extend that same care and compassion to their students. It's a ripple effect—and it starts with leadership.

Well-supported teachers are more patient, more reflective, and more willing to lean into relationship-centered practices rather than survival-mode teaching. When leadership normalizes rest, boundaries, and honest conversations about burnout, it shifts the culture from endurance to sustainability.

Make Families Feel Welcomed

Relationships with students are strengthened when you also build relationships with their families. Create a school culture where families feel genuinely welcomed—not just tolerated.

This goes far beyond having an "open door policy" that exists in name only. It means critically examining how you communicate with families, when and how meetings are scheduled, and what unspoken assumptions might be keeping parents and guardians at a distance. Too often, we unconsciously operate from a deficit mindset about family involvement—assuming that if parents aren't present, they don't care. The reality is, many families are juggling multiple jobs, navigating systemic barriers, or carrying their own difficult histories with school systems that failed them. It's our job as educators and leaders to meet them where they are—not just physically, but emotionally and culturally.

That might mean offering flexible meeting times, sending messages in multiple languages, hosting community events in accessible locations, or simply picking up the phone to share a positive story instead of only calling when there's a problem. It also means consistently and visibly inviting families into the school building—not just for emergencies or performances, but as regular partners in their child's education. When students see their families and teachers working together, on the same team, something powerful happens. They feel a greater sense of belonging, accountability, and motivation. They thrive.

When families feel respected rather than judged, communication becomes proactive instead of reactive. Trust built with caregivers strengthens the relational bridge around the child, reinforcing the message that school and home are united in belief and purpose.

We have to dismantle the stigma that parents are only needed when something goes wrong. The truth is, they are the first teachers. They are the constant in a child's life, while staff and classrooms may change year to year. When we embrace parents as equal partners—not as guests or observers—we build a network of support that holds students up and pushes them forward.

Welcoming families into the building with warmth and purpose helps cultivate trust, dismantle barriers, and signal to students that their full identity—their home, their culture, their people—is respected and valued in our school community.

Use Data to Tell the Relationship Story

Yes, test scores matter. But they're not the only data that tells the story of your school's success. Academic achievement is only one piece of the puzzle. If we want to understand what truly drives sustainable success in schools—particularly for students who are historically marginalized—we must start paying attention to *relational data* as well.

Track indicators like:

- **Student attendance rates:** Consistent attendance is a strong sign that students feel safe, welcome, and connected to school. When students have positive relationships with staff and peers, they are more likely to show up—even when life outside of school is difficult.
- **Discipline referrals and suspension data:** When relationships improve, behavioral incidents often decrease. Fewer office referrals signal that students are feeling more supported, that adults are de-escalating rather than punishing, and that classroom communities are rooted in trust, not control.
- **Student survey responses:** Directly ask students how they feel. Do they feel like they belong? Do they feel like at least one adult in the building knows them well? Do they feel safe, respected, and seen? These responses can uncover truths that academic data alone cannot.

- **Family engagement levels:** Are families attending events, responding to communication, and feeling like authentic partners? Increased family participation often reflects a stronger sense of trust between school and home.
- **Teacher retention rates:** Schools that prioritize strong, positive staff-student relationships also tend to support and retain teachers. When teachers feel like their relational work is valued—and when they witness its positive impact on student behavior and performance—they are more likely to stay.

When you track these indicators over time, patterns begin to emerge. Schools with intentional relationship-building practices often experience:

- Higher attendance
- Decreased behavioral issues
- Stronger academic performance
- Greater student voice and engagement
- Higher staff morale and retention

This data becomes your evidence. It becomes your *why* when advocating for the time, professional development, and resources needed to support relationship-centered practices. It shifts the narrative from "this is nice, but optional" to "this is essential to our school's success."

The more we center relational data in school improvement conversations, the more we can build learning environments that are truly holistic—where every student, educator, and family feels connected, valued, and empowered to thrive.

Be Patient with the Process

Culture change doesn't happen overnight. Some teachers will embrace relationship-building immediately; others will need time and support to get there. Some students will be eager to connect; others will test you to see if you're really committed to this approach.

Stay the course. Celebrate the small wins. Learn from the setbacks. And remember that every authentic relationship built in your building is an act of resistance against a system designed for some students to fail.

The Bottom Line

As a school leader, you have the power to create conditions where every student feels seen, valued, and supported. You can build a culture where relationships aren't just nice to have—they're the foundation of everything you do.

But it requires intentionality, courage, and a willingness to prioritize what truly matters. It means being willing to push back against policies and practices that prioritize compliance over connection. It means choosing love over fear, relationships over rules, and students over systems.

The students in your building are counting on you to make that choice. Don't let them down.

The Choice Is Yours

Every morning when you walk into your school building, you carry with you the power to change a life. It might be the struggling reader who needs to know that smart comes in many forms. It might be the class clown who's using humor to mask pain. It might be the quiet student in the back who has brilliant ideas but has never felt safe enough to share them.

The barriers are real. The system pushes against you. Time feels scarce, and the pressure to focus on test scores can feel overwhelming. But in the midst of all that noise, there's a simple truth that cuts through everything else: relationships save lives.

The truth is, you have to be willing to do the Heart Work. You have to be invested in a vision that maybe no one else can see, and you have to put yourself in a position to be vulnerable even when student behavior may tell a different story. This isn't about naive optimism or ignoring reality—it's about understanding that beneath every defensive posture, every act of defiance, every shutdown moment, there's a human being who needs to feel valued and seen.

The truth is, people thrive in environments that offer safe spaces. This isn't just educational theory—it's human psychology. The truth about the streets is that everyone bonded over one thing: the need to feel valued. When young people can't find that sense of belonging and worth in our classrooms, they'll find it elsewhere. And sometimes "elsewhere" becomes a place that validates them in ways that ultimately harm them.

I think about my interview from Controversial Conversation with Dr. Peay. His story haunts me because it represents a failure of our educational system to provide what he desperately needed: authentic connection and recognition of his worth. I think about all the students I've worked with over the years who were one relationship away from a completely different story. One adult who saw past their behavior to their potential. One teacher who refused to give up when everyone else had written them off.

And I think about the educators I've trained who've told me, "This changed everything for my students and me." They discovered that when you show up authentically, when you do the Heart Work of truly seeing your students, when you create spaces where young people feel genuinely valued—everything shifts. Behavior improves not because of consequences or rewards, but because students finally have something worth protecting: a relationship that matters.

This is why Heart Work is non-negotiable. It requires us to be vulnerable, to invest in relationships that may not immediately show returns, and to believe in possibilities that others might not see. But when we commit to this level of authentic connection, we create the conditions where students don't just survive—they thrive.

The research is detailed and as clear as it can be: students perform better academically when they feel connected to school. They're less likely to drop out, less likely to engage in risky behaviors, and more likely to pursue their dreams when they have at least one adult who believes in them unconditionally.

But this isn't just about data and outcomes. This is about humanity. This is about seeing the child behind the behavior, the potential behind the struggle, the brilliance behind the barriers. This is about choosing to be the adult you needed when you were their age.

As school leaders, we must create cultures where relationships aren't just encouraged—they're expected, where teachers feel supported in truly knowing their students. Where love isn't seen as soft, but as the strongest foundation we can build.

As educators, we have the privilege of being the person who sees a student's light when they can't see it themselves. Of being the voice that says, "You matter. You belong. You have something important to offer this world."

The student in your classroom tomorrow might be the next great teacher, innovative scientist, or compassionate leader our world needs. But they'll only become that person if someone—maybe you—takes the time to build a relationship that helps them see their own potential.

Within an education system that hasn't historically supported all students equally, choosing to build authentic, caring relationships with every child isn't just good teaching—it's revolutionary. It is an act of defiance against low expectations, against bias, and against the belief that some children are worth more than others.

Every relationship you build is a vote for equity. Every connection you make is a step toward justice.

But relationships do not stop at the classroom door. For students to truly thrive, schools must recognize families as partners—not obstacles.

The truth is simple: relationships save lives.

This work requires a willingness to do the Heart Work—to invest in a vision that others may not yet see, and to remain open even when student behavior tells a different story. This isn't naive optimism. It's the understanding that beneath every defensive posture, every act of defiance, there is a human being searching for value and belonging.

As educators and leaders, we have the privilege—and the responsibility—to be the adults who see a student's light when they cannot yet see it themselves.

The choice is ours.

And the students are waiting.

✧ **Pause & Reflect**

Saving Students One Relationship at a Time

Schools often emphasize outcomes—grades, test scores, attendance, and performance metrics. Yet behind every measure of success is something far less visible and far more powerful: relationships. Students do not fully engage in spaces where they feel unknown, misunderstood, or disconnected. Trust is not a program or an initiative; it is built moment by moment through consistency, empathy, and presence.

This chapter reminds us that relationships are not secondary to instruction—they are the condition that allows instruction to matter. When students believe they are valued, they are more willing to persist, to repair mistakes, and to see themselves as capable learners.

Building those connections requires intentional effort. It asks educators to reflect not only on how they reach students easily, but also on where connection has been difficult and why.

Consider:

- Which relationships in your educational journey helped you thrive, and what made those connections meaningful?
- Where do you find it easiest to build rapport, and where does it feel more challenging?
- How might stress, assumptions, or time pressures influence the way relationships are formed or avoided?
- What signals do students receive about belonging through everyday interactions in your learning environment?

Leadership Lens:

How does a school's structure—schedules, expectations, and priorities—either protect time for relationship-building or unintentionally push it aside?

A Small Shift:

Choose one student, colleague, or family member to engage with more intentionally this week. A brief moment of genuine attention can begin to rebuild connection and trust.

"The people closest to the problem are closest to the solution—but often farthest from power."

— Gloria Ladson-Billings

Chapter Eight
The Power of the Parent Card

Introduction

Close to the end of this book, I decided that it was now or never. For years, I'd felt the pull toward something greater—something that allowed me to make an impact beyond the limits of a system that had long since lost its way. Deep down, I knew my time as an employee in traditional education was coming to an end. I had played the game, followed the rules, and watched as politics and policy overshadowed purpose. I could no longer ignore the truth—the system was designed to keep itself intact, not to transform.

I had been standing at a crossroads for quite some time. After taking a major leap to start my own business years prior—and watching it not unfold as I hoped—I retreated to reflection and healing. I spent years analyzing missteps, unpacking trauma, and slowly rebuilding my confidence. Each step reminded me that I deserved more: more alignment, more authenticity, and more freedom to lead with heart.

When I finally decided to invest in a coach, one of the first requirements was to take a DISC assessment. At first, I thought, *What does this have to do with fixing my business?* But soon it became clear. The assessment forced me to confront the gap between who I naturally was and who I had been trying to be in professional spaces. As an employee, I had learned to suppress my voice to appear more "collaborative," but in truth, I was diluting my power. The burnout was real, and the cost was clarity.

The assessment was more than just a personality quiz—it was a mirror. It forced me to confront the uncomfortable gap between who I naturally was and who I had been performing as in professional spaces. The DISC assessment gave language to what I was experiencing. It showed me where my natural tendencies lay—my drive, need to be seen as autonomous, unique, independent, and to stand apart from the crowd—and highlighted how much energy I was spending trying to override those instincts in a work environment that didn't value my natural talents. Instead of fixing my business, I realized the work began with fixing my relationship with myself. I needed to reclaim my voice, honor my strengths, and build a business that reflected who I truly was, not who I thought I needed to be to make others comfortable.

That moment was a turning point. By embracing my authentic self, I found a new sense of clarity and direction—not just for my business, but for my life.

Then came the experience that shifted everything. It did not arrive dramatically or with warning. There were no flashing lights announcing transformation—just a quiet heaviness in my spirit that told me something inside me could no longer bend without breaking.

I had a meeting with a parent, a return conference following her child's suspension. I was already uneasy, recalling a difficult interaction with her the previous year. The student's behavior had been deteriorating, and despite my efforts to partner with the mother, she repeatedly rescheduled our meetings. I tried everything to convey that our shared goal was her child's success, but nothing seemed to resonate.

Too often, parents believe schools either condone or are responsible for "fixing" behaviors that originate at home. But educators are not miracle workers—we are extensions of the foundation built by parents. When that partnership breaks down, so does the support system a child desperately needs. And when trust erodes, children learn quickly whom to divide and how to survive within the fracture. They sense tension before adults name it. They adapt to dysfunction long before anyone addresses it.

As I sat across from that family, I saw generations of pain and misunderstanding colliding. A grandmother who had normalized ignorance. A mother who mirrored it. A child who absorbed it. There was no accountability—only blame.

The air in the room felt thick with defensiveness. Every statement became a shield. Every suggestion became an attack. No one was listening to understand; they were listening to defend. What could have been a moment of collective growth became another example of how systemic failure repeats itself through silence and misunderstanding.

She had pushed away the very person who believed her child could succeed—someone who saw beyond the misbehavior, the tantrums, the class disruptions, and the disrespect. I didn't see a "problem child." I saw potential trapped beneath patterns of pain. I saw a child who needed boundaries, love, and consistency, and a mother who was too wounded by her own experiences to see that I was not the enemy. That moment broke something in me—but it also opened my eyes. I realized I had been fighting battles that were never mine to carry alone. I had mistaken responsibility for ownership. I had absorbed outcomes that required collective courage, not individual sacrifice.

In that moment, I felt both heartbreak and clarity. I realized that my ability to create meaningful change within the system had reached its limit. I could no longer pour from an empty cup or fight battles on uneven ground. The imbalance had become unsustainable. The expectation to produce transformation without authority, reform without resources, and partnership without reciprocity had drained whatever margin I once had. The system had taken everything it could from me, but it could not take my purpose.

That meeting marked my pivot point—the moment I decided to shift my focus toward advocacy, empowerment, and education beyond the classroom. If I wanted to make a real difference, it would have to be on my own terms—through partnership, truth-telling, and a deep commitment to helping parents understand their power in shaping the lives of their children. It meant stepping outside the walls that had once defined my identity. It meant risking misunderstanding. It meant choosing impact over security and purpose over predictability.

Because the truth is this: parents hold more power than they realize. In a system intentionally designed for some to succeed and others to fail, parental advocacy is not just influence—it's disruption. When parents are informed, engaged, and unafraid to question the status quo, they become the most powerful force for equity that schools cannot ignore. Their voices can shift narratives, their persistence can dismantle barriers, and their presence can redefine what accountability looks like. Systems shift when pressure becomes consistent. Narratives change when silence is replaced with strategy. Power redistributes when those once dismissed decide they will no longer wait for permission.

Parental advocacy, when rooted in knowledge and courage, is the lever that can move even the most entrenched institutions.

So to every parent reading this: know that your questions matter, your presence matters, and your persistence is a catalyst for change. The system will not shift on its own. It shifts when you decide to act, together.

The educational system may be structured to maintain control, but the collective power of parents—especially those from marginalized communities—has the potential to upend that design. True reform begins when schools stop seeing parents as obstacles and start seeing them as partners. That is where transformation happens. That is where liberation begins.

Let's be Real

In every school community, there is one powerful force that is often underestimated, overlooked, or engaged only when there's a problem: parents. Not because they lack influence, but because their influence is rarely activated strategically. Their presence is felt, but their power is not always cultivated. And that difference matters more than most people realize.

Working in urban schools over the years, I've learned that the difference between a student who struggles in silence and one who thrives often lies in whether or not there's a parent—or guardian—actively involved, informed, and connected to what's happening inside the school. The "Parent Card," when played intentionally and proactively, is one of the most powerful tools in the education system. But far too often, it only gets pulled when a crisis emerges. By then, conversations are defensive instead of collaborative. The focus shifts from growth to damage control. Opportunities that could have been addressed early become conflicts that feel urgent and overwhelming. A behavior issue. A suspension. A failing grade. And by that point, emotions are high, facts are muddy, and trust is fractured. Everyone enters the room carrying assumptions. Teachers feel scrutinized. Parents feel judged. Students feel exposed. The environment becomes charged before a single productive sentence is spoken.

I've worked with countless parents who only show up when their child is in trouble. Not because they don't care—but because they don't know. They are unaware of the language educators use. They don't know the policies shaping decisions. They don't know how early intervention could shift outcomes long before a report card ever reflects a problem. They're often ill-informed, disconnected from the day-to-day realities of school, and unsure how to advocate effectively. And truthfully, schools haven't always made it easy for them to be involved. We say we want partnership, but sometimes we communicate like we want compliance. We say "parents welcome," but our systems say "only if you follow our rules."

This chapter isn't about blaming parents—or educators. It's about building bridges. It's about understanding the power of collaboration between school and home. It's about shifting from reactive to proactive engagement. Students begin to feel supported from every direction. Expectations become consistent across environments. Accountability feels shared rather than imposed. When parents are equipped with knowledge, when relationships with teachers are rooted in trust, and when schools truly embrace families as partners, everything changes—for the better.

Section One: The Impact of Proactive Parent Engagement

When parents and caregivers are involved proactively—not just when things go wrong—students benefit in ways that data alone can't fully measure. They feel supported, seen, and valued from every angle. That consistency builds emotional security. It tells a child that the adults in their life are aligned—not divided—and that their growth is a shared priority. The message becomes clear: *"I matter enough for my school and my family to work together."*

Research has consistently shown that students with engaged families are more likely to:

- Attend school regularly
- Earn higher grades and test scores
- Have better social skills and behavior
- Graduate from high school and pursue post-secondary education

But engagement can't be reduced to a quarterly parent-teacher conference or an occasional flyer sent home in a backpack. Real engagement requires intentional relationship-building, mutual respect, and shared responsibility for student success. It requires conversations that go beyond grades and behavior. It calls for listening as much as advising, understanding as much as instructing.

When schools proactively reach out—*not* just when a child is failing or misbehaving—they signal to families that their voice matters. And when parents make the effort to stay informed, build relationships with their child's teacher, and stay connected to the school community, they become powerful advocates who can help ensure their child's needs are being met.

This collaboration doesn't just support academic success—it also creates a safety net for students. A child who knows their parent and teacher are in consistent communication is less likely to fall through the cracks. They are more likely to course-correct early, to seek help without shame, and to internalize the belief that support is always within reach. The accountability is clear, and the sense of support is strong.

In underserved communities, where families have often been excluded from decision-making or made to feel unwelcome in school spaces, this kind of partnership becomes even more critical. It's not about checking a box—it's about shifting the culture.

Section Two: The Problem with Reactive Engagement

The foundation of strong parent-school relationships begins *before* there's a problem. One of the most powerful steps a parent can take is to meet their child's teacher at the start of the school year. That initial connection sets the tone for open communication, mutual respect, and trust. It transforms future conversations from introductions into continuations. When familiarity exists, even difficult discussions feel less adversarial and more solution-oriented. It tells the teacher, *"I'm here. I care. I want to be involved."* And it tells the child, *"We're in this together."*

Too often, though, schools don't create enough accessible opportunities for families to meet teachers early, or parents don't realize how important that early connection really is—until something goes wrong.

I've worked with many parents who only engage when their child is in trouble. They come into the building frustrated, sometimes angry, with little understanding of what's actually happening in the classroom. The blame gets passed around, and the conversation becomes about the behavior, not the child. The problem isn't that these parents don't care—it's that they've been conditioned by their own school experiences to only be called in when there's an issue.

This reactive approach serves no one. It turns what could have been preventative dialogue into crisis management. Instead of building a strategy together, both sides scramble to defend their positions. When the first real interaction between school and home happens under stressful circumstances, it creates a barrier to trust. Parents feel defensive. Teachers feel unsupported. And students feel caught in the middle.

But when relationships are built early—when teachers take time to get to know families, and families make time to get to know teachers—problems can be addressed collaboratively, not combatively. The conversation shifts from blame to solutions. Energy that once fueled tension begins fueling progress. The focus returns to growth, not fault.

Early relationship-building helps prevent misunderstandings. It humanizes everyone involved. It opens the door for parents to ask questions, share insights about their child, and become part of the team from day one.

Because here's the truth: teachers and families *are* on the same team. The mission is shared, even when methods differ. Alignment does not require uniformity—it requires commitment to the same outcome. But if we don't establish that partnership early, it's easy to end up working in opposition—especially when emotions are high, and communication is lacking.

Section Three: Closing the Communication Gap

Communication is the bridge between school and home, and when that bridge is broken or shaky, everyone suffers—especially students. One of the most common issues I've witnessed in schools is the communication gap between educators and families. Sometimes, it's due to language or cultural barriers. Other times, it's because schools only reach out when something goes wrong. And too often, it's because systems are reactive instead of intentional. Policies may exist, but consistency in outreach does not. Communication tools are available, yet they are not always used to foster connection before conflict.

This communication gap leaves parents feeling disconnected and uninformed. They may hear about a behavior issue, a missing assignment, or a failing grade long after it could've been prevented. When parents don't know what's happening in their child's academic life, they're forced to make decisions and form opinions based on partial information. That's where the breakdown begins. Assumptions fill the silence. Narratives are created without verification. Trust erodes not because of one incident, but because of accumulated gaps.

The Cultural and Class Divide

The communication gap often widens along cultural and socioeconomic lines. Schools may communicate in ways that assume certain cultural knowledge or availability that not all families possess. Automated calls in English only, emails sent during work hours, or meetings scheduled without considering work schedules all contribute to excluding certain families from the communication loop. These practices may appear neutral on the surface, yet they quietly privilege families with flexible time, language fluency, and access to technology. Equity in communication requires more than equal effort—it requires intentional accommodation.

Some parents may feel intimidated by educational jargon or formal communication styles, which can cause them to avoid reaching out even when they have concerns. In other cases, they may reach out only after frustration has built up, and that frustration can come across as anger. Meanwhile, schools may misinterpret these reactions as hostility or lack of interest rather than recognizing them as signs that families feel unheard or disconnected. What looks like disengagement is often discomfort. What appears to be anger can sometimes be the result of parents feeling that their concerns were not acknowledged earlier.

This is not to say that all anger is misinterpreted. But as educators, we must learn to recognize the signs beneath the surface. Sometimes parents are simply looking for reassurance—confirmation that their child is seen, supported, and valued. And what appears to be silence is sometimes uncertainty about whether their voice will truly be heard.

The Child's Perspective

Children are acutely aware of this communication breakdown, and it affects them deeply. They may feel caught between two worlds that don't seem to understand each other. In that tension, children often carry emotional weight that was never meant for them. They internalize conflict that adults have yet to resolve. Some children learn to manipulate the gap, telling different stories to parents and teachers. Others become anxious, knowing that problems are building but unsure how to bridge the divide between home and school.

The Path Forward

Breaking this cycle requires intentional, systematic changes to how schools approach family communication. It means moving from reactive communication (only when there's a problem) to proactive communication (regular updates on progress and concerns). It means recognizing that communication is not just about delivering information—it's about building relationships and trust. Information can be transmitted in seconds. Trust is cultivated over time. One informs; the other transforms.

Most importantly, it means acknowledging that when communication fails, it's not because parents don't care or teachers don't try hard enough. It's because we haven't created systems that prioritize ongoing, meaningful dialogue between the adults who care most about each child's success.

Parents deserve regular, honest communication—not just about what their child is doing wrong, but about what they're doing well. Affirmation builds confidence, not only in students but in families. When strengths are acknowledged, conversations about growth feel balanced rather than punitive. They deserve to be included in conversations about their child's academic growth, behavioral patterns, and social-emotional development. When families are informed, they are better positioned to advocate for their children and partner with schools to ensure success.

Likewise, teachers need communication from parents, too. Families offer insight into their children's interests, fears, habits, and experiences. When that information is shared early and openly, it helps teachers build stronger relationships, design more relevant instruction, and anticipate challenges before they escalate.

The key is consistency. Schools must commit to frequent and varied methods of communication—phone calls, newsletters, parent-teacher conferences, text messages, class apps, and even home visits when appropriate. Not every family engages in the same way, so schools must be flexible and culturally responsive in their communication strategies.

But it's not just about how we communicate—it's also about the *tone*. Too often, school communication feels one-sided or transactional. True partnership begins when educators speak with families, not at them. It grows when we approach each other with empathy and shared purpose. Parents should never feel like outsiders in the education of their own children. When schools intentionally dismantle that perception, they transform from institutions of authority into spaces of shared stewardship.

When we close the communication gap, we don't just keep families informed—we empower them.

Section Four: Advocacy Begins with Awareness

True advocacy isn't about showing up only when there's a problem—it's about staying informed, engaged, and proactive in your child's educational journey. It's about knowing your rights as a parent, understanding your child's needs, and working collaboratively with educators to ensure those needs are met. Advocacy is both posture and practice. It's the quiet confidence that comes from preparation, and the steady persistence that follows when conversations become uncomfortable. It requires discernment—knowing when to listen, when to question, and when to insist.

Many families assume that advocacy only comes into play during disciplinary issues or academic failure. But advocacy starts much earlier—it begins with awareness, whichis preventative. It allows you to notice patterns before they become labels. It gives you the language to describe concerns before they escalate into consequences. Knowing how your child learns best, being familiar with school policies, understanding how to navigate school systems, and being able to identify when something doesn't feel right are all critical aspects of advocacy.

One of the simplest yet most powerful advocacy actions you can take is *meeting your child's teacher early and often*. The beginning of the school year sets the tone. That first connection with the teacher matters. It communicates that you're engaged, invested, and willing to collaborate. Teachers, despite what some may believe, welcome this kind of partnership. Most educators enter this profession because they care deeply about children. When families approach with collaboration rather than confrontation, it creates space for mutual respect instead of defensiveness. When parents and educators are on the same page, it makes the work smoother and more meaningful—for everyone involved.

Advocacy also means *asking questions* and staying in the know. Read the school's code of conduct before you sign it. Attend parent-teacher conferences, even if you need to request a phone call or Zoom meeting instead. Check the school website for updates. Review report cards and behavior reports closely. Ask for clarification when things don't make sense.

You have a right to know what's going on in your child's learning environment, and your child has the right to have someone advocating for what they need to thrive. Silence rarely protects a child. Questions do. Presence does. Clarity does. The more informed you are, the less likely it is that decisions will be made about your child without you. That might mean requesting academic accommodations, inquiring about differentiated instruction, or making sure your child has access to resources that align with their learning style. It might also mean raising concerns when something feels off—or unfair.

But advocacy isn't always about raising red flags. Sometimes it's about strengthening the relationship before there's tension. Sometimes it's about creating goodwill that makes future conversations easier to navigate. It's also about *offering support*. Ask your child's teacher if there's anything you can do to assist. Maybe you have a special skill or hobby you can share with the class. Maybe you're available to help with an event or a project. Maybe you just want to show up and be present in the building, helping to create a stronger sense of community. Any time you contribute in this way, you reinforce the message that you are an active partner in your child's education.

When parents advocate—not just in times of crisis, but consistently—they help create schools where students feel supported, where teachers feel valued, and where collaboration becomes the norm rather than the exception. Consistent advocacy normalizes involvement. It removes the stigma that engagement equals conflict. It reframes participation as a partnership.

Your presence matters. Your voice matters. And when those two are aligned with strategy, they carry influence. Advocacy without preparation can feel chaotic. Advocacy grounded in knowledge feels steady and effective. When you combine awareness with action, you become the kind of advocate who makes a real difference.

I remember working with a parent whose child attended a primarily white school district. The teacher had created a narrative that her child was the problem - the disruptive one, the difficult one, the one who couldn't follow directions. But as this mother shared her experiences with me, I could see that things had been blown completely out of proportion. There were simple solutions to the challenges her child was facing, solutions that should have been obvious to any experienced educator. But when assumptions precede understanding, clarity gets clouded. Bias narrows vision. And what could have been resolved through curiosity becomes complicated through perception.

That's when it hit me: sometimes when bias is at play, we as educators become the problem. At the end of our conversation, I knew with certainty that this teacher could not possibly have a real relationship with this child. How could they? They had reduced him to a collection of behaviors rather than seeing him as a whole person.

As an educator myself, the solutions were so clear to me. I told this mother that at her next meeting, she needed to go above and beyond to discuss her child's likes, dislikes, personality traits - everything that made him who he was. She needed to force that teacher to see the individual, not just the 'issue.' Because once you truly see a child, the solutions follow easily. When you understand a child's motivations, strengths, and triggers, intervention becomes personalized rather than punitive. Strategy replaces speculation.

Fast forward, the parent let me know that she felt empowered. The approach was effective, and although the relationship between her child and the teacher didn't turn around right away, they were making real progress. We then discussed what communication would look like moving forward and practical ways for her to stay on top of what was happening in the classroom.

This is what parent advocacy looks like when it's strategic rather than reactive. It is measured, not explosive. It is prepared, not impulsive. It centers the child while addressing the system. It's not about being confrontational—it's about being informed, intentional, and persistent. It's about refusing to accept that your child is 'the problem' when the real issue might be an adult's inability to see past their own bias.

I understand how frustrating it can be when you're dealing with behavioral and academic challenges. Sometimes parents become emotional, and those emotions can put them in a state where they're unable to hear the facts clearly or advocate effectively for their child. Sometimes they're frustrated because they feel the school doesn't have their child's best interests at heart. There are so many reasons why emotions can mask the real concern. Emotion often signals attachment, not irrationality. It reveals how deeply a parent cares, even if the delivery lacks polish.

Sometimes schools assume that if parents are not as visible or involved as they could be, it means they don't care. But that assumption can be misleading. In my consulting work, I've learned that care often runs much deeper than what schools see on the surface. If you "poke the bear," you quickly realize just how much parents care. When a parent feels that their child is being treated unfairly or overlooked, that protective instinct can surface quickly. The mama bear is ready to fight for her cub—and in that moment, the school can easily become the perceived enemy.

But here's what I've learned through my consulting work: underneath all that emotion—the anger, the frustration, the tears—parents are usually trying to communicate something much deeper. They're saying, *"I don't feel like you know my child." "I don't feel like my child is a priority." "I don't feel like I'm being supported." "I don't feel like you're on our side."*

When we pause long enough to listen beyond the emotion, we often discover that what parents truly want is partnership, reassurance, and the confidence that the adults responsible for educating their child genuinely care about their success.

When parents understand this about themselves, they can move from emotional reactions to strategic action. Instead of letting frustration drive the conversation, they can address the real issue: the lack of relationship and understanding between the school and their child. This shift from reactive to strategic advocacy changes everything - for the parent, for the child, and often for the school's response. It changes the tone of meetings. It changes the questions being asked. It changes the assumptions that shape outcomes.

But here's what I learned from working with this mother: most parents don't know they have this power. They've been conditioned to defer to educators, to accept whatever narrative the school creates about their child. They don't realize that sometimes, the most loving thing they can do is push back. Push back with preparation. Push back with documentation. Push back with clarity about what their child deserves. Advocacy is not opposition—it is protection guided by purpose.

Section Five: The Parent Card as Resistance

When schools dismiss parent advocacy as "playing the parent card," they're actually revealing their discomfort with informed, empowered families who refuse to accept the status quo. But what if we reclaimed that phrase? What if playing the parent card meant strategically using your knowledge, your voice, and your love for your child to disrupt a system designed for some students to fail?

A Step-by-Step Guide for Parent Advocates

When schools dismiss parent advocacy as "playing the parent card," they're actually revealing their discomfort with informed, empowered families who refuse to accept the status quo. But what if we reclaimed that phrase? What if playing the parent card meant strategically using your knowledge, your voice, and your love for your child to disrupt a system designed for some students to fail?

Here are the essential steps every parent needs to follow when advocating for their child:

STEP 1: KNOWLEDGE AS POWER

The first step in effective parent advocacy is understanding that you have rights—and knowing exactly what they are. Through my consulting work, I've seen how quickly the dynamic changes when parents walk into meetings armed with knowledge instead of just concerns.

What You Need to Know:

Your Legal Rights:

- IDEA (Individuals with Disabilities Education Act): If your child has or might have a disability, you have the right to request evaluations, participate in IEP meetings, and ensure your child receives a free and appropriate public education.
- Section 504: Protects students with disabilities from discrimination and ensures they have equal access to education through accommodations.
- Title IX: Protects against sex-based discrimination, including sexual harassment and gender-based bullying.
- Title VI: Prohibits discrimination based on race, color, or national origin in federally funded programs.

School-Specific Policies:

- Your district's discipline policy and appeals process
- Grading practices and grade change procedures
- Academic placement criteria and challenge processes
- Bullying and harassment reporting procedures
- Parent complaint and grievance policies

The Power Shift:

When you understand these rights, you move from asking ("Could you please help my child?") to asserting ("My child is entitled to..."). This isn't about being confrontational—it's about being informed. Schools are required to follow these laws, and when parents know them, it forces schools to justify their decisions rather than just implement them.

Action Steps:

- Research your state's Department of Education website for parent rights documents
- Request copies of all relevant school policies
- Join parent advocacy groups or online communities for your area
- Consider consulting with education advocates or attorneys for complex issues

STEP 2: STRATEGIC COMMUNICATION

Advocacy without documentation is just conversation. But advocacy with a paper trail? That's power.

Document Everything:

Meeting Notes:

- Date, time, location, and attendees at every meeting
- Specific statements made by school personnel
- Decisions reached and next steps agreed upon
- Any promises made by school staff

Written Communication:

- Save all emails to and from school personnel
- Follow up verbal conversations with email summaries: "As we discussed today..."
- Keep copies of all letters, forms, and official documents
- Screenshot text messages if that's how your school communicates

Incident Documentation:

- Date, time, and details of any concerning incidents
- Names of witnesses
- Photos of injuries, damaged property, or relevant evidence
- Your child's account of what happened

The Power of Written Requests:

Always put your requests in writing and ask for written responses; this can be done by writing an email. This creates accountability and shows you're serious about your concerns. Instead of saying, "Can you help my child with reading?" write: "I am requesting that my child receive additional reading support. Please provide me with a written plan detailing what interventions will be implemented and how progress will be measured."

Communication Best Practices:

- Use professional, respectful language even when frustrated
- Be specific about what you want and when you need it
- Copy relevant administrators on important emails
- Set reasonable deadlines for responses (usually 5-10 business days)
- Follow up if you don't receive responses within your timeframe

STEP 3: DISRUPTING LOW EXPECTATIONS

The most dangerous thing a parent can do to an inequitable system is refuse to accept low expectations for their child.

Challenge Academic Placement Decisions

Come Armed with Data:

- Your child's test scores, grades, and work samples
- Evidence of your child's abilities outside of school
- Research on best practices for your child's learning needs
- Examples of successful interventions from other schools or districts

Question the Criteria:

- "What specific criteria are you using to make this placement decision?"
- "How does this placement align with my child's demonstrated abilities?"
- "What data supports this recommendation?"
- "What would my child need to demonstrate to be placed in a higher-level class?"

Demand Culturally Responsive Practices

Know What to Look For:

- Curriculum that reflects diverse perspectives and experiences
- Teaching methods that connect to your child's cultural background
- Discipline policies that don't disproportionately affect students of color
- Staff who understand and value your child's cultural identity

Ask the Right Questions:

- "How are you incorporating my child's cultural background into their learning?"
- "What training has the staff received on culturally responsive teaching?"
- "How do you ensure that discipline policies are applied equitably?"
- "What steps are you taking to address any racial disparities in academic outcomes?"

Challenge Discipline Policies

Understand the Pattern:

- Request data on suspension and expulsion rates by race and ethnicity
- Ask for information about alternative discipline options
- Understand your child's rights during disciplinary proceedings
- Know the difference between minor infractions and serious offenses

Advocate for Restorative Approaches:

- "What restorative justice options are available instead of suspension?"
- "How will this consequence help my child learn and grow?"
- "What support will be provided to address the underlying issues?"
- "How will you ensure my child doesn't fall behind academically during any disciplinary action?"

STEP 4: THE RIPPLE EFFECT

When one parent successfully advocates for their child, they're not just changing one student's trajectory—they're creating pathways for other families to follow.

Build Parent Networks

Connect with Like-Minded Parents:

- Attend school board meetings and PTA/PTO events
- Join or create parent advocacy groups
- Use social media to connect with other parents facing similar challenges
- Share resources and strategies with other families

Collective Action:

- When multiple parents have the same concern, present it together
- Coordinate meeting attendance to show unified support
- Share the workload of researching policies and solutions
- Amplify each other's voices in public forums

Create Lasting Change

Policy-Level Advocacy:

- Attend school board meetings to address systemic issues
- Submit formal complaints to district offices or state departments of education
- Work with local advocacy organizations to push for policy changes
- Run for the school board or support candidates who share your values

Mentoring Other Parents:

- Share your knowledge and experience with newer advocates
- Help other parents understand their rights and options
- Provide emotional support during difficult advocacy journeys
- Celebrate victories together and learn from setbacks

Document Success:

- Keep records of positive changes that result from your advocacy
- Share success stories (with permission) to inspire other parents
- Create resources and guides for other parents to use
- Build a reputation as a knowledgeable, effective advocate

STEP 5: CONNECTION TO YOUR CENTRAL MISSION

In a system designed for some students to fail, parent advocacy isn't just about getting what your child needs—it's an act of resistance. It's truth-telling in action. It's refusing to be complicit in your child's educational oppression.

Advocacy as Resistance

Challenge the Status Quo:

- Refuse to accept "that's just how we do things" as an answer
- Question policies and practices that don't serve your child
- Demand transparency in decision-making processes
- Hold schools accountable for equitable treatment of all students

Truth-Telling in Action:

- Name bias and discrimination when you see it
- Share your experiences with other parents and community members

- Speak up at public meetings about systemic issues
- Use your voice to advocate for students whose parents may not be able to

Building Equity:

- Advocate not just for your child, but for all children facing similar challenges
- Push for policies that benefit marginalized students
- Support other parents in their advocacy efforts
- Work toward systemic change that creates equity for all students

Your Legacy:

Every time you advocate for your child, you're modeling for them that their voice matters, their education is important, and they deserve to be treated with dignity and respect. You're also paving the way for other parents to find their voice and fight for their children.

Remember:

- You are your child's first and most important advocate
- You have the right to be heard and respected
- Your advocacy can create change that benefits many students
- Persistence and strategy are more effective than anger and confrontation
- You are not alone in this fight

The Power is in Your Hands:

When you play the parent card strategically, you're not just advocating for your child—you're disrupting a system that depends on parent silence and compliance. You're demanding that schools live up to their promise of educating all children. You're refusing to let your child be another casualty of educational inequity.

That's not being difficult. That's being revolutionary

Section Six: Shifting the Narrative

For far too long, the narrative around parents—especially parents from historically marginalized communities—has been laced with deficit thinking. Phrases like *"they don't care," "they're never involved,"* or *"they're hard to reach"* echo in staff lounges and leadership meetings across the country. These stereotypes not only misrepresent families, but they also actively harm school culture and relationships. Deficit language becomes self-fulfilling. When we lower expectations of families, we lower the quality of invitation. And when an invitation lacks authenticity, engagement declines—not because families don't care, but because they sense they are not truly valued.

We need to shift the narrative. And narrative shifts begin internally. They begin in the private conversations educators have with one another. They begin in the assumptions we challenge within ourselves before we ever address them publicly.

The truth is, many parents *do* care deeply, but they've been made to feel unwelcome or undervalued in school spaces. They've had negative experiences with education—either as students themselves or through past interactions with their child's school—and they carry that history with them. In some cases, language barriers, work schedules, lack of transportation, or simply not knowing the "right" questions to ask can all become barriers to visibility, not to engagement. Visibility and engagement are not the same. A parent may not be physically present in the building, yet still be deeply invested at home. We must be careful not to equate presence with care.

Schools must stop framing absence as apathy. Absence often has context. It has history. It has an explanation. When we pause to understand the why, we often uncover effort that simply looks different from what we expected.

Parents are our students' first teachers. They are experts on their children in ways that educators will never be. And when schools approach families as true partners rather than passive participants—or worse, problems to manage—the impact is transformational. Power shared does not weaken institutions; it strengthens them. Collaboration does not create chaos; it cultivates clarity.

Shifting the narrative means creating *authentic entry points* for families to be involved. Entry points that do not require perfection. Entry points that do not demand familiarity with educational jargon. Entry points that honor lived experience as expertise. It means valuing their voices in decision-making, respecting their time, and welcoming their presence not just for disciplinary meetings or fundraisers, but for everyday learning. It means asking, *"How can we bring parents in?"* rather than assuming they won't show up.

It also means rethinking what parent engagement looks like. It doesn't have to be a PTA meeting or a bake sale. Engagement might be a parent emailing a teacher to ask how their child is doing. It might be a guardian calling the school to request extra support with homework. It might be a caregiver who shows up after working a night shift just to watch their child read a poem in class.

These acts deserve just as much recognition as the traditional forms of involvement. Engagement should not be measured by visibility alone. It should be measured by intention, effort, and impact on the child.

And just as importantly, educators need to stop treating advocacy as antagonism. Discomfort does not equal disrespect. Questioning does not equal defiance. Sometimes what feels challenging is simply accountability arriving at the door. When a parent questions a grade, asks about an assignment, or pushes for services, it's not an attack—it's advocacy. When parents advocate, they're not challenging your authority—they're stepping into their power. And when schools embrace that power instead of resisting it, students win. And power, when aligned with purpose, is not threatening—it is constructive. It creates shared responsibility rather than silent resentment.

The new narrative must reflect this truth: families are not outsiders to education—they are essential to it, not just in theory, but in practice. Not as symbolic participants, but as active contributors whose insight shapes outcomes. Their engagement is not a bonus—it's a necessity. And their voices should never be silenced—they should be centered.

We don't shift narratives by wishing. We shift them by examining bias where it hides. By interrupting deficit talk when it surfaces. By choosing language that reflects possibility instead of presumption. We shift them by doing the work: listening, reflecting, changing our language, and changing our systems.

The question is not whether families want to be involved. The question is whether schools are willing to make space for them to lead, to question, to collaborate—and to help create the schools their children deserve. Making space requires surrendering control. It requires reimagining leadership as shared stewardship. It requires courage to admit that families may see what institutions have overlooked.

Section Seven: Reclaiming the Parent Card

The term *"parent card"* is often used flippantly—invoked when a parent steps in to speak on their child's behalf, to question a policy, or to push back on something that feels unjust. But the truth is, the parent card is powerful, and when used intentionally, it can shift the entire trajectory of a child's school experience. Power, when misunderstood, is often labeled as disruption. But disruption is sometimes necessary when systems have grown comfortable with inequity. The parent card unsettles patterns that no longer serve children—and that is precisely why it matters.

To reclaim the parent card is to reject the idea that schools know best *without* parents. For too long, expertise has been narrowly defined as credentials rather than lived experience. Yet no degree replaces the daily knowledge a caregiver holds about their child's temperament, strengths, fears, and resilience. It is to stand in the power of your voice and say, *"I deserve to be here. I know my child. And I will show up, ask questions, and expect answers."*

When parents reclaim their rightful place in the educational journey, schools transform. Meetings become dialogues instead of monologues. Policies are examined instead of blindly enforced. Decisions begin to reflect collaboration rather than hierarchy.

Reclaiming the parent card means:

- Showing up—early, not just when there's a problem.
- Asking the hard questions—even when they make people uncomfortable.
- Learning the system—so you can work it, challenge it, and change it.
- Speaking up for your child—especially when no one else will.
- Partnering with teachers—not from a place of blame, but from a shared belief in your child's potential.

It also means documenting conversations. Keeping records. Following up in writing. Understanding timelines and escalation processes. Advocacy is most effective when it is both relational and strategic. It means understanding that your presence sends a message—not just to the school, but to your child: *"I believe in you, and I am invested in your success."* That message becomes internalized. Children who witness their parents advocating learn self-advocacy. They learn that their voice carries weight. They learn that silence is not their only option.

When schools and families work together in true partnership, our children thrive. They feel supported, protected, and empowered. They know there is a village behind them. And when a child feels backed by a united front, confidence replaces isolation. Resilience replaces shame. Belonging replaces fear. And that village becomes a force stronger than any test score, suspension, or stigma they might face.

The parent card isn't about control—it's about collaboration. Collaboration does not eliminate disagreement. It reframes it. Disagreement handled with respect becomes refinement. Resistance handled with openness becomes reform. Control seeks dominance. Collaboration seeks alignment. One protects the ego; the other protects children. It's about stepping into the room, not to demand perfection, but to demand care, equity, and accountability.

And when more parents feel empowered to play that card, and more educators feel ready to receive it with openness and respect, we don't just change outcomes. Mutual readiness is critical. Advocacy cannot flourish in environments where questioning is punished or where dialogue is perceived as defiance. We change lives.

Let's stop treating the parent card like a last resort. It should not appear only in moments of crisis. It should be woven into everyday engagement—normalized rather than sensationalized. Let's recognize it for what it is: a powerful act of love, advocacy, and resistance. Resistance rooted in love refuses complacency. It refuses to accept narratives that limit children's potential. It insists on systems that respond rather than dismiss.

Fighting for children—your own and others—comes at a cost. Emotional labor accumulates. Meetings stretch beyond school hours. Mental energy is spent anticipating resistance. Advocacy requires stamina, and stamina requires support. Advocacy without boundaries leads to exhaustion, especially for Black educators expected to carry more with less support. Too often, the expectation is silent: to translate systems, mediate conflict, mentor families, and absorb institutional tension without acknowledgment. The burden becomes normalized, and the toll becomes invisible. Reclaiming the parent card must also include reclaiming sustainability. Advocacy is not martyrdom. It is not self-erasure. It is purposeful engagement rooted in clarity, not constant depletion.

When parents organize collectively—sharing information, supporting one another, attending meetings together—the parent card multiplies in strength. Individual advocacy influences classrooms. Collective advocacy reshapes policy.

Reclaiming the parent card is not about creating division—it is about restoring balance. It is about remembering that education was never meant to be a one-sided exchange, but a shared responsibility rooted in trust and mutual accountability. When families and schools operate in isolation, children feel the fracture. But when adults choose alignment over ego, collaboration over control, something powerful begins to shift.

True partnership requires humility from educators and courage from parents. It requires both sides to move beyond defensiveness and toward dialogue. It asks us to see each other not as obstacles, but as allies bound by a common purpose. Because at the center of every policy, every meeting, every difficult conversation, there is a child watching and learning what advocacy looks like.

When parents remain informed, when teachers remain open, and when communication remains consistent, the system begins to reflect the people it serves. Children grow up understanding that their voices matter because they have seen the adults in their lives use theirs wisely. They learn that accountability and compassion can coexist. They learn that community is not accidental—it is built.

And when that happens, education becomes more than instruction. It becomes a partnership in its truest form.

✧ **Pause & Reflect**

The Power of the Parent Card

Advocacy often begins in moments of discomfort. A grade that doesn't sit right. A disciplinary decision that feels unfair. A meeting that leaves more questions than answers. In those moments, families must decide whether to remain silent or speak up.

The "parent card" is not about conflict. It is about clarity. It is about refusing to allow confusion, bias, or low expectations to go unchallenged. It is about remembering that partnership requires participation.

Strong school-family relationships are built on trust, transparency, and mutual respect. But when trust is fractured, advocacy becomes necessary.

Before moving forward, take a moment to reflect:

Consider:

- When have you felt unheard or dismissed in a school setting?
- How did that experience shape your trust in educators?
- If you are an educator, how do you typically respond when a parent challenges a decision?
- Do your systems make it easy or difficult for families to ask questions?
- What assumptions might you carry about "involved" versus "uninvolved" parents?

Leadership Lens:

How does your school communicate expectations, policies, and decision-making processes? Is the information accessible, clear, and equitable for all families — or only for those already familiar with the system?

A Small Shift:

Choose one interaction this week — with a parent, caregiver, or guardian — and approach it with intentional curiosity instead of assumption. Lead with listening. Clarify before correcting. Partner before defending.

"Black educators never give up!!! There are going to be some tough days, days when you feel like throwing in the towel, but don't because it will always be students that will appreciate what you are doing. And even the students that give you a hard time will remember at least one thing that touched and helped them!!!!"

-Vontella Moye

Educator

Chapter Nine
Burnout, Boundaries, and Black Joy

Right now, I'm writing this chapter in my backyard on a warm, breezy Sunday evening, eating peach cheesecake (a new flavor from The Cheesecake Factory) and sipping wine called The Sweetest Thing from a nearby winery in Ellicottville. The sun is setting just right, the air feels soft, and for once—I'm not rushing to do anything else. I've never felt more at peace. For a long time, peace felt unfamiliar to me—almost suspicious. Like something that would disappear if I relaxed too much. So I'm learning to sit in it without waiting for the other shoe to drop. And no, everything in my life is not perfectly figured out. There are still emails in my inbox. People had things for me to do today. But I stuck to what I had planned instead. And guess what? That's not selfish—it's necessary. It's called boundaries. It's called choosing yourself, your time, and your joy.

I've been looking forward to writing this chapter. Deep down, I knew this one would feel different. I knew the words would come easily, because they're real. What I have to say here will resonate with so many people—especially those who are holding everything together while quietly falling apart. The ones who smile through meetings, show up for everyone else, answer every call, and carry the weight without complaint. The ones who keep moving, keep giving, and then allow the exhaustion and despair to wash over them when no one is watching.

Yesterday, I had an epiphany: happiness is voluntary. It's a choice. Not because life is easy. Not because the struggle disappears. But because I finally realized that my response belongs to me. You can choose to be happy—even in the midst of struggle. I was presented with a challenge that almost pulled me out of character. I felt those big feelings (as Ms. Rachel would say), and I almost reacted out of frustration. I almost let it ruin my day. My chest tightened. My thoughts sped up. The old version of me was ready to react immediately. But I paused. I've been doing the inner work. I've been learning to move strategically in the direction that points to the best version of me. I sat back, analyzed my emotions, validated what I was feeling, and chose happiness anyway. It felt liberating.

As a Black woman, it often feels like I carry the weight of the world. I'm the responsible one, the go-getter, the fixer, the queen of solutions. But the weight gets heavy. Heavy in my shoulders. Heavy in my decisions. Heavy in the expectation that I will always figure it out—no matter what it costs me. And in my forties, I finally started to question: Who signed me up for this? And more importantly, why did I keep renewing the contract?

I wasn't sure how I got here, but I knew one thing for certain—I couldn't stay there. I realized I didn't need permission to be happy. I didn't have to earn joy. My world wouldn't fall apart just because I took a moment to breathe.

For a long time, I believed happiness was dangerous. I convinced myself the only way to keep everything from unraveling was to stay alert—always ready for the next challenge, the next problem, the next crisis. I was living in a constant state of fight or flight, and I thought it was normal. I thought exhaustion meant I was ambitious. I thought anxiety meant I was responsible. I thought constant alertness meant I was strong.

But strength isn't living in survival mode.

Strength is choosing peace.

Boundaries: The Choice to Reclaim Yourself

Here's what I've learned the hard way: people will only do what you allow. That's not just a cliché—it's a life lesson that often comes at a cost. And for me, that cost almost came in the form of a mental breakdown. Not the dramatic kind you see in movies. The quiet kind. The kind where you're still showing up, still smiling, still answering emails—while your nervous system is screaming for relief.

And if I'm being honest, there was a point where I was angry. I wanted to fight. I was hurt. I was disappointed in myself for always taking the high road. For staying quiet when I should have spoken up. For trying to be the bigger person while quietly carrying the weight of other people's behavior.

Because here's the truth nobody likes to say out loud: if you never point out the wrongs done to you, people will keep crossing the line. Some will even convince themselves that you were okay with it. That you didn't mind. That you somehow liked it.

Silence can easily be mistaken for permission.

And I had been silent for far too long.

I was new to administration and finally starting to find my rhythm. I had a team under me that was committed, passionate, and ready to do the work. We weren't just colleagues—we were a unit. We built a school culture rooted in support, trust, and family. Parents trusted me. Teachers felt seen and supported. The work felt meaningful, and it showed. I wasn't just managing systems—I was nurturing people. I knew their strengths. I knew their struggles. I knew which teacher needed encouragement and which one just needed space. Leadership, for me, was never about power. It was about stewardship.

But the success we built wasn't celebrated by everyone. At first, I tried to ignore the subtle shifts. The shorter emails. The meetings I suddenly wasn't invited to. The energy in the room that felt… different. I told myself I was overthinking it.

My supervisor—someone with more positional power—began to resent the relationships I had nurtured. The same connections that made our school strong became a threat to her control. Right before COVID-19 hit, we had a team of professionals come in to conduct observations. We were up for renewal, and their goal was to assess our progress and recommend next steps.

After three days of interviews, classroom visits, and deep listening, they came back with a single, resounding conclusion: **I needed to be empowered to lead.** They said I should be given full authority to carry out the vision I had already begun putting into motion.

You would have thought that would be a turning point.

And in a way, it was—just not the one I expected. Because what followed wasn't empowerment. It was a performance. It was optics. It was the illusion of collaboration without the substance of trust.

My supervisor pretended to be on board. This person nodded in agreement, smiled in meetings, and even gave the illusion of including me in key decisions. But when it came to real follow-through? Nothing. No invitations to leadership meetings. No voice in decisions that directly affected the school community. And worse—their attitude toward me began to shift. The coldness. The condescension. The subtle undermining. Comments disguised as "feedback." Decisions made without context. Conversations about me instead of with me. It was psychological warfare dressed up as professionalism. The lies she hid behind from the comfort of her office, while I was expected to carry out harmful directives that would erode the very relationships I worked so hard to build.

Emails came down ordering me to enforce policies that made no educational sense—rules that were intentionally designed to strain the trust I had with my staff. It was sabotage in slow motion. My sleep changed. My appetite changed. I would wake up at 3 a.m. replaying conversations in my head, wondering what I could have done differently. I started shrinking in rooms I once felt confident in. I began to push back, to challenge her. And from there, the relationship became toxic. Unhealthy. Emotionally abusive.

What I endured during that time—if I listed it all—most people would struggle to believe it. But it happened. And eventually, the stress became unbearable. I took time off, as ordered by my doctor. I transitioned to working from home. I felt like I was unraveling. Not because I wasn't capable—but because I was carrying too much without protection. I had mastered resilience, but I had never learned how to rest inside it.

Then something changed.

Boundaries Are a Love Language

I sat down with a Black woman doctor—someone who knew exactly what it meant to carry the weight while also being expected to smile through it. She didn't sugarcoat anything. This wasn't a conversation for the phone. She looked me in the eye and said:

"You have more education than this person. You have more insight. You turned that school around with limited experience. And you have the power to take control of your life at any given moment. There is no reason for you to keep living like this. Depression is real—but so is choice. You don't need permission to be done. *You* hold the cards. The only question is: what do you want to come from this?"

That conversation changed me. It woke me up.

Because here's the truth: we stay in places too long. Jobs. Relationships. Situations that deplete us. We convince ourselves we have no choice when, in fact, we do. We always do.

At any moment, we can choose to walk away from what doesn't serve us. We can choose joy over performance. Peace over proximity. Integrity over approval.

I didn't need permission to protect my peace. I needed to reclaim it.

Boundaries aren't walls—they are declarations of self-worth. And in a profession that demands so much—our time, our hearts, our energy—we must learn to say: *Enough. I matter too.*

You can care deeply about the work and still say no to what harms you. You can be committed to students and still protect your mental health. You can love education and still leave toxic systems behind.

You don't have to prove your value to people who benefit from undervaluing you.

The day I chose myself was the day I began to heal. This was a turning point in my life, not just my career.

From Survival to Joy

When I arrived at this chapter, I had every intention of sharing the emails, naming names, and calling everything out. I wanted to expose the harm. I drafted the paragraphs in my head. I rehearsed the receipts. I imagined the validation that might come from telling the full, unfiltered truth. For a moment, that felt satisfying.

But the truth is—I'm not the judge or the jury. And I'm no longer the woman I was back then.

Back then, I led with urgency. With defense. With the need to prove myself.

Today, I lead with clarity. With discernment. With peace.

Even now, I could write an entire chapter about a more recent experience. I walked into that situation with full transparency. I shared what I had been through before. I believed honesty would create a different outcome. I thought maybe this time would be a fresh start.

But sometimes the lesson repeats itself.

And I've learned something else along the way: not every experience deserves a permanent place in your story. Some people simply aren't worth the ink on the page.

For me, this is growth.

These experiences don't discourage me. They sharpen me. They remind me to move differently, to trust my instincts, and to honor what I already know about my own worth.

I'm not angry.

I'm focused.

I'm not questioning my abilities.

I'm aligned.

Because when you truly know your worth, you stop fighting for spaces that were never designed to see it.

Today, I'm a more grounded, more polished version of who I used to be. I am still learning this version of myself, and sometimes that growth is uncomfortable. But I refuse to go back.

For me, growth was quiet. It didn't come with an announcement or applause. It happened in the small decisions—choosing peace over reaction, clarity over chaos, and boundaries over burnout.

I've learned to be intentional about where and how I spend my energy. And trust me, this person doesn't deserve an ounce of it.

My energy is sacred now. It fuels my purpose, my creativity, and my peace. I no longer donate it to dysfunction.

I'm not sharing this story to relive the pain or reopen old wounds. I'm sharing it because it represents a turning point, a moment that forced me to confront the difference between surviving and truly living.

This story isn't about them—it's about what happens when you decide you deserve better.

It's about choosing joy, even when the world gives you every reason not to.

Joy is not denial. It is defiance. It is the quiet rebellion of choosing light in spaces that profit from your burnout. It is the act of reclaiming your peace in a profession that often demands your entire soul.

And once you experience that kind of clarity, there is no going back.

Education is a field that will take everything if you let it. It applauds sacrifice but rarely models sustainability. It praises passion but doesn't always protect the passionate. We give our all. We show up early, stay late, lose sleep, skip meals, and carry the burdens of other people's children on our backs. We absorb their trauma. We advocate through systems that don't always listen. We pour from cups that are already running low. And yet, we don't always get to see the fruits of our labor. Sometimes the seeds we plant take a decade to bloom. Sometimes you never see the bloom at all. You just trust that your presence mattered in ways that statistics can't measure.

But then—one day—you run into a former student whose face lights up just at the sight of you. Or the child who was once labeled "behavioral" is now thriving in a career they love. Or a teacher pulls you aside and says, "Thank you for seeing me when no one else did."

That's why we do this. That's the return on the investment. Not the titles. Not the recognition. Not the politics. The impact. The legacy. The lives quietly shaped because you showed up consistently.

So no, I won't waste time dragging the bosses I've had who tried to dim my light. I'm too busy walking in joy, choosing peace, too busy building environments where people feel safe, too busy modeling boundaries that my younger self didn't know were allowed, and being the version of myself that younger me needed—and that today's students and educators deserve.

Advice for the Reader

I know there's someone reading this right now who has their own story. Maybe you're in the thick of it—worn out, overlooked, questioning your worth. Maybe you've normalized the exhaustion. Maybe you've convinced yourself this is just what leadership feels like. Maybe you're smiling publicly and breaking privately. I won't tell you to just "stick it out." What I *will* say is: go where you are valued. Not tolerated. Not barely acknowledged. Not used. Valued. There is a difference. Such places do exist.

Take the time to weigh your pros and cons, and then make the decision that best serves *you.* You owe yourself that much. You owe yourself clarity. You owe yourself honesty. You owe yourself the kind of future that doesn't require you to shrink to survive.

Rest when you're tired. And I don't mean some once-in-a-while kind of rest—I mean unapologetic, non-negotiable rest. A nap should not feel like a luxury. You are not a machine. You are not a crisis-response unit. You are a human being whose nervous system deserves calm.

If your plate is too full, say so. You don't need a dramatic breakdown to justify stepping back. You don't need visible exhaustion to prove you've earned a pause. Set the boundary. People will continue to pile things on until you do. And when you finally choose yourself—when you show up unbothered, peaceful, and unavailable for the chaos—yes, some people will be mad. Let them be. Their disappointment is not your emergency. Their discomfort is not your assignment.

Pay them no mind. Silence can be powerful. So can peace. Not every battle requires your participation.

Go to work. Mind your business. Protect your peace. And most importantly, continue to pour into *yourself.*

Every. Chance. That. You. Get.

Read the book. Take the walk. Schedule the therapy session. Book the trip. Sit in silence. Do the thing that reminds you who you are outside of what you produce.

You are not here to burn out. You are here to live fully, love deeply, and move through this world as your whole, healed self. Don't let anyone convince you otherwise. Not a supervisor. Not a system. Not even your own fear.

Burnout forces a reckoning. It strips away the performance. It exposes what you've been tolerating. It asks hard questions about access, boundaries, and belief. It asks us what we are willing to give—and what we must protect to keep going.

At some point, you will have to decide whether you want to be admired for your endurance or respected for your boundaries. One will drain you. The other will free you. Choose wisely.

Closing Reflection:

Burnout has a way of making you question everything—your purpose, your passion, even your place in the profession. When you've given so much of yourself for so long, it can feel like there's nothing left to give.

But the truth is, many of us are still here.

Despite the exhaustion.

Despite the frustration.

Despite the moments when walking away felt easier than staying.

We are still here because somewhere along the way, a student reminded us why the work matters. A breakthrough moment. A quiet thank you. A small victory that no one else noticed but meant everything to the child who experienced it.

Those moments have a way of pulling us back to our purpose.

Choosing joy doesn't mean ignoring the challenges of this profession. It means refusing to let those challenges define your entire story. It means learning to protect your peace while still holding space for the work that matters.

Because when educators begin to reclaim their joy, set boundaries, and reconnect with their purpose, something powerful happens: the work becomes sustainable again.

And that raises an important question.

If this work can be so difficult—so demanding, so emotionally heavy—why do so many of us stay?

The answer to that question is where our story goes next.

✧ **Pause & Reflect**

This chapter explored the emotional weight many educators carry—the pressure to keep going, to keep giving, and to keep holding everything together even when you feel like you're falling apart. Burnout doesn't always show up as collapse. Sometimes it shows up as quiet exhaustion, constant tension, and the feeling that you are pouring from an empty cup.

Take a moment to reflect on your own experience.

Reflection Questions

- Have there been moments in your career where you felt emotionally or mentally drained but continued pushing forward anyway? What kept you going?
- In what ways have you prioritized the needs of others while neglecting your own well-being?
- How comfortable are you with setting boundaries in your professional life? What makes that difficult?
- What are the signs that you may be operating in "survival mode" rather than thriving?
- When was the last time you experienced genuine joy in your work? What contributed to that moment?
- What would it look like to reclaim space for your own peace, creativity, and purpose?

Burnout often convinces us that slowing down is failure. In reality, reflection is one of the most powerful forms of renewal. Taking time to acknowledge your experiences allows you to reconnect with the purpose that brought you to this work in the first place.

Next Steps

Burnout does not happen overnight, and healing from it doesn't either. Reclaiming your well-being requires intentional choices about how you show up in your work and in your life. The goal is not to care less about students—it is to care about yourself enough to remain whole while doing the work you love.

Consider the following steps as you move forward:

1. Recognize the signs of burnout early.

Pay attention to emotional exhaustion, constant irritability, feeling detached from your work, or losing the sense of purpose that once motivated you. Awareness is the first step toward change.

2. Set and protect professional boundaries.

You cannot pour endlessly into others without replenishing yourself. Establish limits around your time, your emotional energy, and your responsibilities. Boundaries are not selfish—they are necessary for sustainability.

3. Prioritize your mental and emotional wellness.

Whether it's journaling, therapy, exercise, prayer, meditation, or time spent with loved ones, invest in practices that restore your sense of balance and peace.

4. Redefine what success looks like.

Success in education is not measured by how much you sacrifice. It is measured by the impact you make while maintaining your humanity and well-being.

5. Protect your joy.

Joy is not a luxury—it is a form of resistance. In a profession that can easily consume your energy, choosing joy is an act of self-preservation and strength.

6. Seek supportive communities.

Surround yourself with people who understand the emotional demands of this work and who encourage your growth rather than drain your energy.

Burnout may be part of the story for many educators, but it does not have to be the ending. When you learn to protect your peace, honor your boundaries, and reconnect with the purpose that brought you into education, you begin to move from survival to renewal.

And from that place, the work becomes sustainable again.

"If you don't like something, change it. If you can't change it, change your attitude."

— Maya Angelou

Chapter Ten
What Keeps Us Here

You know that feeling you get at the end of the school year—when you look back on everything you've been through and realize none of it overshadows what you've accomplished? The year is ending, your students are moving on, and your heart is full of both pride and ache. It's emotional. Not just for you, but for them, too. You were their second home for eight hours a day. You loved them, taught them, nurtured their minds. And now, your only hope is that you've given them enough to survive and thrive without you. On to the next chapter—for them, and for you.

You pack up bulletin boards, take down the posters that once framed their curiosity, and quietly fold away the little pieces of a year that meant more than anyone outside that room will ever fully understand. The desks will soon belong to another group of children with new stories, new struggles, and new dreams. But the echoes of laughter, frustration, breakthroughs, and growth will always live in the quiet corners of that classroom.

This is the final chapter of this book, but it's not the end of the journey. Because education is never just about the year that ends, it's about the invisible threads we leave behind in the lives of students long after they walk out of our classrooms. Seeds planted in moments that felt ordinary at the time but later bloom into confidence, courage, and possibility.

We're still here. Still showing up when the systems feel broken.

Still believing that what happens between four classroom walls can change the trajectory of a life.

Still carrying the quiet hope that one caring adult can become the difference a child remembers forever.

There are so many reasons I'm still passionate about education—and yet, there are just as many reasons why I could have walked away. This profession is not for the weak. It requires patience that stretches beyond exhaustion, compassion that survives disappointment, and a resilience that must be rebuilt again and again. Every lesson plan carries more than academic goals—it carries the weight of shaping futures.

And for educators of color, it often feels like a battleground. Not because we came looking for conflict, but because simply existing with confidence, excellence, and authenticity can challenge systems that were never designed to celebrate us. Every day becomes an act of perseverance. We show up day after day, ten toes down, teaching content while simultaneously proving our worth in spaces that profit from our presence but were never built with us in mind.

Yet even in those moments, we keep showing up. Not because the system suddenly becomes easier, but because the work inside the classroom still matters too deeply to abandon. The students sitting in those desks are not responsible for the limitations of the systems that surround them. They arrive each morning with curiosity, questions, struggles, and dreams that deserve to be nurtured. And for many of them, the classroom becomes one of the few places where their voice can be heard and their potential recognized.

Too often, we are hired for what we represent rather than what we can truly do. We're expected to manage behavior, to be relatable to the students, and to serve as visible symbols of diversity on a website or in a brochure. A team of highly educated and talented Black principals presented as a powerhouse for publication purposes—yet stripped of the ability to make real decisions behind closed doors.

If the walls of our offices could talk, they would tell the story of the constant balancing act: trying to show up authentically while navigating the unspoken politics of the system. The tension of knowing you are capable, prepared, and often more than qualified, while also being aware that pushing too hard or questioning too much can suddenly shift how you are perceived.

The reality is that many of us are constantly calculating—carefully deciding how much of our voice to use, how much truth to speak, and how far we can push against the grain without triggering discomfort from those in power.

And the moment we step outside the narrow box we were placed in and begin to advocate, question, or lead boldly, the narrative changes.

We are no longer seen as an asset.

We become the problem.

Teaching, at its heart, is an act of belief. It is the belief that a child who struggles today may discover their strength tomorrow. It is the belief that encouragement offered in a quiet moment can echo in a student's life long after they have forgotten the lesson itself. And it is the belief that representation, compassion, and consistency can shape how young people see themselves in a world that may not always affirm their worth.

For educators of color, this belief carries an additional layer of purpose. Our presence alone can expand what students imagine is possible. When they see someone standing confidently in front of the room—someone who understands their experiences, their culture, or their challenges—it sends a message that cannot be captured in any curriculum guide. It tells them that their story matters, that their voice belongs in spaces of leadership, and that their future holds possibilities far greater than the limitations others may try to place upon them.

The room grows quieter when truth enters the conversation. Advocacy becomes labeled as an attitude. Passion becomes misinterpreted as defiance. And suddenly, the very qualities that once made you valuable become the reasons you are questioned.

I've seen what jealousy from colleagues and leaders looks like when they can't replicate the magic we create in classrooms and schools. They see the way our students respond to us, how the families trust us, how the community leans on us. And rather than celebrating it, they try to minimize it. But they still need us.

They need the energy we bring into classrooms. They need the connection we build with students who have learned to trust very few people. They need the cultural understanding, the empathy, and the authenticity that cannot be manufactured in policy meetings or professional development sessions. They'll keep us around just long enough to benefit from our presence. And then they'll act shocked when we've had enough.

I've witnessed so much in this profession. More than I ever expected. Things that could break even the strongest among us. To love what you do and still feel your spirit slowly being drained by toxic systems—it's a kind of heartbreak I wouldn't wish on anyone.

But something keeps pulling us back, because I have also seen through those heartbreaks and through those difficult moments that could break anyone—I have seen the moments of incredible beauty and moments of deep injustice. Breakthroughs that made me believe in miracles and obstacles that made me question whether the system would ever truly change. Maybe it's the memory of a student who once said, "You're the only teacher who believed in me." Maybe it's the quiet understanding that what we do matters even when no one writes it in a report or measures it on a test score.

We get up and teach like our lives depend on it. Because in some ways, they do. Because for some of our students, the classroom is the safest place they know.

Because for others, it is the only space where their voice is heard, and their potential is recognized.

Because we love what we do—and more importantly, we love who we do it for.

We love the messy, unpredictable, human work of helping young minds grow. The work that rarely gets applause but always leaves fingerprints on the future.

We stay for the student who finally read a full book for the first time.

For the kid who couldn't sit still in September but is now leading group discussions in May.

For the parent who calls to say thank you, not because everything was perfect, but because you tried.

You tried for the quiet student who may never say it out loud but carries your encouragement into every challenge that comes next. For the moments years later when a former student walks up to you and says, "You changed my life," and suddenly every difficult day makes sense.

For the colleague who pulls you aside and says, "Because of you, I didn't quit."

Because sometimes the work is just as heavy for the adults as it is for the students. The long days, the quiet frustrations, the moments when you wonder if the system will ever see the effort you pour into it. And in those moments, knowing that your presence helped someone else keep going becomes its own kind of strength.

We stay because it matters. Because the classroom is more than a workplace—it is a place where futures quietly take shape. Where confidence grows in small, almost invisible ways. Where a single conversation, a moment of encouragement, or a belief spoken at the right time can follow a student for the rest of their life.

And even when we leave the classroom, many of us never leave the work. Whether we become consultants, administrators, professors, or policy advocates, we find ways to keep pouring into students, into communities, into the future. Our roles shift, but the mission remains. The work simply takes on a different form. Instead of guiding students directly, we begin shaping the environments around them—building systems, writing policies, mentoring educators, and advocating for changes that classrooms have needed for generations.

Yes, we could leave. Many of us have. Many of us will. Some days, the thought crosses our minds more than we'd like to admit. When exhaustion settles into our bones, and the weight of expectation feels heavier than the support surrounding us. But there's something deeply rooted in this calling. It grows from the belief that education is one of the most powerful tools a person can carry into the world. And once you've seen what it can unlock in a child, it becomes impossible to completely turn away from it. A purpose. A fire that doesn't burn out—it just flickers on hard days and reignites with every student success, every lesson that lands, every moment when a student's eyes light up because something finally made sense. Those small victories that rarely make headlines but mean everything inside the classroom. Every hug in the hallway, every "You were my favorite teacher."

To be a Black educator in this system is to resist every day. It means carrying pride in who we are while navigating spaces that sometimes question our presence. It means standing firm in our identity while still holding space for the growth and well-being of the students who look to us for guidance. It's to show up in truth, to bring love into rooms where it was never part of the curriculum, to create environments where students feel seen, respected, and valued—not just for their academic performance, but for who they are as people, and to demand better—for our students, for ourselves, and for those who will come after us.

This work requires more than professional skill; it requires courage. Courage to speak when silence would be safer. Courage to advocate for students whose brilliance may be overlooked. Courage to remain rooted in dignity even when the system fails to recognize it. Each day we step into the classroom, we carry not only our expertise, but also the quiet determination to ensure that every child who walks through that door knows they belong there.

We don't stay because it's easy. We stay because it's meaningful. In fact, there are many days when the path would be far simpler if we walked away. But purpose rarely chooses the easiest road. Purpose often asks for persistence when recognition is scarce and the work feels unseen. It calls us to remain steady when doubt creeps in, and systems feel immovable. Yet the deeper truth of education is this: transformation rarely happens in comfort. It happens through patience, consistency, and a belief in the possibility that refuses to disappear.

Meaning lives in the small moments most people never see—the student who finally raises their hand after weeks of silence, the young mind that begins to trust its own voice, the quiet realization that someone believes in them. These moments may never appear in data reports or policy discussions, yet they are the heartbeat of education.

And when we do leave—because boundaries are healthy, because rest is necessary, because our wellness matters—we don't leave empty-handed. We carry with us the memories of the lives we touched and the lessons those students unknowingly taught us in return. We leave with our heads high, knowing we made a difference. That our presence mattered. That the hours spent planning, encouraging, correcting, and believing were never wasted. That the seeds planted in those classrooms will continue growing long after we are gone. That our voice echoed. That our light—though dimmed at times—never went out. Because the work of an educator is never confined to a single classroom or a single year. It travels quietly through the lives of students who carry forward the confidence, encouragement, and belief they once received. Long after names fade from attendance rosters, the influence of a teacher continues shaping decisions, dreams, and possibilities. Because the impact of an educator doesn't end when the school bell rings for the last time. It continues in every student who walks forward carrying a piece of what they learned—not just from the lessons, but from the person who believed they could succeed.

In closing, I want to leave you with this:

I see you. I appreciate you. And so do your students.

Even on the days when the appreciation isn't spoken aloud. Even when the impact of your work feels invisible in the moment, the seeds you plant in young minds have a way of growing quietly long after the classroom door closes.

We are in this together. We are committed to being the difference—but on our terms. We are the difference. Not because we claim perfection, but because we choose presence. Because we bring humanity, empathy, and persistence into spaces that often measure success only through numbers and outcomes. What we bring to the table is invaluable. The cultural wisdom, lived experiences, and textbooks or policy manuals cannot replicate a deep understanding of our students' realities. It is the kind of knowledge that transforms classrooms into communities. It's pure gold. Don't let anyone dim your light. There will always be voices that try to convince you to shrink, to quiet down, to blend into systems that prefer compliance over courage. But your light was never meant to be hidden. Never compromise your authentic self. Be bold. Be boundaried. Be brilliant.

Stand firmly in the truth of your purpose. Protect your peace as fiercely as you protect your students. And never forget—your presence in this profession is not accidental. It is necessary.

Staying is not passive. It is an intentional act of strength. A daily decision to keep pouring into students, even when the system makes that choice more difficult than it should be. It is a choice—one rooted in courage, conviction, and clarity about what matters most. A clarity that reminds us why we began this work in the first place—because we believed children deserved someone who would fight for them.

"The classroom remains the most radical space of possibility in the academy. For years it has been a place where education could be the practice of freedom. When teachers teach with a commitment to justice and compassion, they create learning spaces where students can grow not only intellectually but emotionally and spiritually.

"In such spaces, education becomes a place of transformation."

—Bell Hooks

Before I close this book, I want to pause for a moment.

Education has never been easy work, and for many of us it has required far more than we ever imagined when we first stepped into a classroom. It has asked us to carry stories that break our hearts, to fight battles that were never written into our job descriptions, and to show up with compassion even when we ourselves were exhausted.

Yet despite all of that, we stayed.

Not because the system made it easy.

Not because the policies always made sense.

Not because the recognition matched the effort.

We stayed because somewhere along the way we discovered that teaching is not simply a profession—it is a form of stewardship. A responsibility to nurture possibility in young people who may not yet see it in themselves.

Every lesson taught, every conversation after class, every moment when we chose patience over frustration—those moments matter more than we often realize. They become part of the foundation students carry with them long after they leave our classrooms.

This book began as a chronicle of truth. But it ends as something more important: a reminder that the work we do as educators carries power far beyond what any system can measure.

And that power lives in you. The conclusion moves us from reflection to responsibility—asking what it means to carry this truth forward with intention. It invites us to consider how our experiences can shape the future of education, and how the lessons we have learned must guide the choices we make from this moment forward.

Conclusion: A Dedication to Educators: A Love Letter in Resistance

Dear Colleagues,

This letter is written with deep respect for the work you carry every day—the visible victories and the quiet sacrifices that rarely receive recognition.

If you've made it to this final page, you've walked with me through every triumph and struggle, every moment of resistance and revelation. You've seen the cost of speaking truth in a system that often prefers silence. You understand the weight that comes with choosing integrity when convenience would have been easier. You've witnessed what happens when we choose students over systems, love over compliance.

Now I need to say something that doesn't get said nearly enough: **Thank you.**

Thank you for the moments when you kept going even when exhaustion told you to stop.

Thank you for choosing this calling, even when the world undervalues what we do. Thank you for showing up every single day for children who need you more than they can express. Thank you for the sacrifices you make that go unseen and unacknowledged. For the emotional energy you pour into children who need stability, encouragement, and hope.

I see you staying late to help the student who's struggling. I see you spending your own money on supplies because you refuse to let your classroom lack what your students need. I see you losing sleep over the child who carries burdens too heavy for their small shoulders. The child whose story stays with you long after the school day ends.

I see you planning lessons at the kitchen table while your family watches TV. I see you making phone calls to parents on your drive home, checking on students who've been on your heart all day. I see you attending professional development on weekends because you believe in becoming better for the children you serve, because growth has always been part of the promise you made to yourself as an educator.

I see you seeing potential where others see problems. I see you believing in students when they've stopped believing in themselves. You become the voice of possibility when the world around them has offered only doubt. I see you being the adult who refuses to give up, even when giving up would be so much easier.

Your work matters. Your dedication matters. Your love for these children matters more than any policy, any mandate, any test score ever could.

But I also know you're tired. Tired of carrying responsibilities that extend far beyond the classroom walls. I know you're frustrated. I know you're watching decisions being made about your students by people who've never stood in front of a classroom. I know you're being asked to implement practices that your gut tells you aren't right for kids. And that internal conflict can weigh heavily on you because you entered this profession with the sole purpose of helping children thrive.

And maybe, after reading my story, you've recognized that moment where staying silent feels like betrayal.

The chronicles you've just read are one educator's journey of resistance—of choosing students over systems, truth over comfort, love over compliance. They're a testament to what happens when you decide that some things are worth fighting for, even when that fight costs you everything.

But this story isn't just mine. It is a reflection of countless educators who have chosen courage when silence would have been safer. It belongs to every educator who has ever felt alone in their convictions. To every teacher who has ever been told they care too much. To every administrator who has ever had to choose between policy and principle.

You are not alone. Your voice matters. Your resistance matters.

The system that tried to silence me is the same system that may be trying to silence you. But here's what I've learned: when we stand together, when we choose truth over comfort, when we put relationships at the center of everything we do—we become unstoppable.

True change rarely begins with permission—it begins with people who are willing to speak, to act, and to lead with integrity.

It's time we stopped fighting these battles in isolation. It's time we united—It's time to support one another in ways that strengthen our collective voice. It's time we stood up for what's right and changed this system from the inside out.

Real change has never come from silence or from individuals working alone behind closed classroom doors. It grows when educators recognize that their shared experiences are not isolated frustrations but collective realities that deserve collective solutions. When we listen to one another, learn from one another, and stand beside one another, we transform exhaustion into solidarity and frustration into action. Community among educators is not a luxury—it is a necessity. In unity, we find the courage to challenge practices that no longer serve our students and the strength to advocate for learning environments rooted in dignity, equity, and opportunity. Together, our voices carry farther than any single voice ever could.

Our students are counting on us. Not just to teach them content, but to model courage, honesty, and compassion. And they deserve educators who are willing to tell the truth, even when—especially when—that truth makes others uncomfortable.

Students notice far more than we sometimes realize. They watch how we respond to injustice, how we speak about fairness, and how we treat every voice in the room. Through these daily interactions, they learn what integrity looks like in practice. When educators choose honesty over convenience and compassion over indifference, we teach lessons that extend far beyond the curriculum. We demonstrate that courage is not always loud or dramatic—it is often quiet, steady, and consistent. By modeling these values, we prepare students not only to succeed academically but to become thoughtful, principled members of their communities.

The chronicles have ended, but your story is just beginning. The resistance starts with you. Every generation of educators inherits both the progress and the unfinished work of those who came before. The responsibility we carry is not simply to maintain the system as it exists, but to imagine how it could be better. That imagination requires reflection, humility, and a willingness to learn from the voices that have too often been overlooked. It asks us to see education not just as a structure, but as a living community shaped by the choices we make each day. When we approach our work with intention and integrity, we help build a future where every student has the opportunity to thrive. And it continues with every educator who chooses to stand in truth, advocate for students, and believe that meaningful change is still possible.

Education has always been about more than curriculum.

It has always been about courage.

The system may try to silence truth, but it can never erase the impact of an educator who chooses to lead with love, conviction, and integrity.

As long as there are educators willing to stand in truth, build relationships, and believe in the brilliance of every child who walks through their doors, the story of education will continue to change.

So keep showing up.

Keep telling the truth.

And keep believing in the power of education to transform lives.

Because truth-telling is not just resistance.

It is how we build something better.

With love, solidarity, and unwavering belief in the power of educators to change the world,

—Dr. Yolanda Peay

Truth-telling is not just resistance.

It is the beginning of change.

www.ingramcontent.com/pod-product-compliance
Lightning Source LLC
Chambersburg PA
CBHW051543050726
47595CB00002B/609